Seasons of Desire

Seasons of Desire

What I Discovered Along the Way

Evelyn D. Klein

North Star Press of St. Cloud, Inc.
St. Cloud, Minnesota

Cover and drawings by Evelyn D. Klein

Copyright © 2012 by Evelyn D. Klein

All rights reserved. No parts of this book may be reproduced electronically or in print without written permission.

Library of Congress Control Number: 2012944756

ISBN 978-0-87839-627-6

First Edition: July 2012

Printed in the United States of America

Published by
North Star Press of St. Cloud, Inc.
P.O. Box 451
St. Cloud, Minnesota 56302

northstarpress.com

For my children, Angie and Bill
and for the journey

Acknowledgments

Grateful acknowledgment is made to editors and publishers for publication of individual poems in the following:

Elements, Minnesota Jung Association, online issue, June 2011: "Mississippi River.

Full Circle, Guild Press, #23: "My Father's World," #25: "The Egret's Return," #26; "Thanksgiving," #27: "In February Light"

Joining the Circle, TA Publications, 2007: "Circle of Renewal"

Moccasin, League of Minnesota Poets, 1987: "Scent of Leaves," 1993: "Summer," 1999: "Spring Winds," 2000: "Invitation," 2001: "The Larger World," "The Melody," 2003: "What My Father Told Me," 2009: "Retreat at Benedictine Center," 2010: "Walk to the Center of the Universe."

Re-Imagining, August 2002:"What My Father Told Me;" May 2003: "Creation"

We Give Thee But Thine Own, House of Hope, October 2004: "Circle of Giving."

    A special thank you goes to my children, Angie Bader and Bill Bader, for their continual support and encouragement in the writing of this book. Thank you, also, to my son for his on-going technological support.

Contents

Introduction xv

I. Road of Seasons 1

Road of Seasons – Press On 4
Seasons 5
Seasons of Hope and Prayer 7
Seasons of a River 9
The Override 10
Music of Ages 11
The Game Along the Way 13
What My Father Told Me 14
To the Muses 15
Circle of Renewal 16
Running for Life 17
The Larger World 19
Skyline of the Faithful 20
Winding Road of Faith 21
Sunday Service 22
All Creatures Bright and Beautiful 23
Timeless 24

II. Spring, Source 25

At Sail 28
Awakening 29
Inspiration 30
Spring Winds 31
The Melody 32
Maundy Thursday 33
The Loss 34
Easter Meditation 35
The Wall and the Vision 36
Resurrection 38
The Egret's Return 39
Promise 40
Mississippi River 41
Nature's Song 42

Prayer 43
Mother's Day Observation 44
Sunshine and Spring Winds 45
Gift of Friendship 46
Pentecost 48
Father's Day Perspective 49
Dedication 50
Coming Home 51
The Robin 52
Picture of My Children 53
Invitation 54

III. Summer, Fountain 55

For Hope 58
To the Sun 59
The Premise 60
In Concert 61
Fourth of July 62
Summer 63
Riding out the Storm at Orchestra Hall 64
The Other Half 65
The Empty House 66
Two Green Apples 67
Mississippi River Bend 68
Shooting Stars 69
Athens Olympics 2004 70
Four in One 71
The Painter 74
Fresh Paint 75
Apollo and the Artist 76
Pilgrimage to Lake Michigan 77
Song of America 78
Well Rooted 81
The Vortex 82
Phoenix Phenomenon 83

IV. Autumn, Gathering 85

At Anchor 88
Autumn 89
River Routes 90
Scent of Leaves 91
Jazz Dreams 92
October Mums 93
Transition 94
Proposal 95
Solace 96
Circle of Giving 97
Perpetual Journey 99
Surprise 101
New Season 102
Halloween Spirits 103
November 104
On Summit Hill 105
Give Us This Day 106
Thanksgiving 108
Union 109
Walk to the Center of the Universe 110
My Father's World 111

V. Winter – Storehouse 113

Crossroads 117
Winter 118
Along the Way 119
Christmas 120
Gifts to My Children 123
New Year's Prayer 125
Out of the Past 126
Toby's on the Lake 127
Visit to Highland Park 128
Snowscape 129
Retreat at Benedictine Center 130
The Labyrinth 131
February Fog 132
Valentine 133
The Plumber 134

In February Light 135
Friendship 136
Lenten Journey 137
Cycle of Creation 138
Finding the Way 139

References 140

The Author 141

*For everything there is a season,
and a time for every matter under heaven . . .*

Ecclesiastes 3

Introduction

Living can be like artistic pursuit. We may know what our goals are, what we want to say in our poems or stories or what we want to show in our pictures. We may even have an idea of how we will get there. But we rarely know exactly what will happen along the way, what we will encounter that we did not anticipate or expect, nor how it will turn out, nor what we will think of it in the end, or if the final results are what we, deep down, really want. Perhaps it turns out better than we hoped for. Perhaps it was the expected, after all. The important thing is to keep moving forward. Life is more than a journey; it is a quest of discovery whether we set out to do so or not. And looking back we stand enlightened in a way that we cannot be when we look ahead.

So many strands of life want to be woven together. It is that which prompted me to write the book. It seems the basis of life is change. It was always there, it seems, but in the twentieth century it began to accelerate, gaining momentum and speed in the twenty-first century to the point where keeping up with change has almost become a way of life. Thus, non-stop days and sleepless nights attest to the fact that we live in a world that never rests and reacts more than it has time to reflect. Scientific advances make many wonder about the religious past and its present traditions. Some question religious notions altogether. Yet evidently human beings have a spiritual side seeking expression, whether we are conscious of it or not. The Swiss psychologist, Carl Jung, points out, it can go underground, if ignored or denied. For me the spiritual, psychological and artistic side of existence form a kind of triangle so intricately connected that it is hard to tell where one starts and the other ends, as the three seem fused into one.

Thus, I chose different forms of expression to give voice to that which needs exploring in different ways and for that which I could find no words. Poetry, with its short lines and rhythm, its succinctness and metaphor is one way to share my experiences and discoveries. Prose is the way I like to examine aspects that invite a more direct approach. Visual art releases the soul to travel with crows in air or with angels in spirit.

The life of the community, the culture and times in which we live, lie at the base of our choices. They influence our thinking and direction, our opportunities and chances for participation and service. They can be static or flexible, progressive or troubled, economically challenged or affluent, professional or blue collar, and so on. In a nation of immigrants, they create diversity and add to change. Of course, while in a mobile society all of this can help open the door to opportunity and lead to progress and growth, it can also make life more involved and complicated, whether professionally, recreationally, or residentially.

In this framework, I am a product of change, where nothing has remained the same from the time of my birth, where every segment of life leads to a new road. At first I saw the changes of our time merely as isolated events, both unfortunate and fortunate, many of which resulted in changes of thinking and new technology, or were part of my education and development, of professional progress applied to motherhood or teaching, of preparing the young for the twenty-first century. But eventually, living the dichotomy of traditional roles and modern profession, I began to realize, after some time of denial and difficulty, that I needed to integrate those changes into my personal life as well and not just apply them as proponent for the future and cheerleader for the young. This new outlook resulted in a renewal of energy and hope, down to the deepest needs and desires, wishes and dreams, perhaps even rekindling those of earlier years. For example, with the birth of my first child, I chose to be a stay-at-home mom. After the children started school, I needed more of a connection to the outside world, and I returned to teaching. Teaching made me a more connected mother, while motherhood made me a better, more understanding teacher. During the years of teaching, I began to write, at first only for professional needs, then creatively, such as poetry, joining writers groups, such as the one I led at the Loft. The writing experience, in turn, helped my teaching and eventually caused me to turn around my days by spending mornings writing and evenings teaching. Writing led to drawing illustrations which added another dimension to my books. Interestingly, I have noticed that some people see me only as my children's mother; others may see me as public school teacher; but those who met me after I published see me as writer, while the artist is becoming an add-on. We all fulfill different roles in our lives. Truth is, each new aspect or vocation added to life overlaps with a previous one, so that we are a composite of all of these.

Hope is the driving force of dreams and goals. It allows us to overcome obstacles of the past and move beyond doubt and fear into new beginnings. The experiences described in this book helped me bridge change and make sense of life beyond random existence and helped me expand my horizon as a person, mother, teacher, and artist. Within the framework of our environment, the greatest power to direct our lives resides within ourselves. Life unfolds a design always in creation and flux, steeped in energy like the long-distance runner to whom each goal becomes both challenge and reward and serves as springboard for the next destination.

I. Road of Seasons

Socrates: . . . "becoming" is by us incorrectly called being, but is really becoming, for nothing ever is, but all things are becoming.

from *Theatetus* by Plato

Sometimes, when I run into someone who looks vaguely familiar, the person turns out to be a former student who, having grown to adulthood, has changed in appearance and manner, leaving only a vague likeness to the younger individual. Invariably, the encounter turns into a lively exchange, a catching up of sorts on college, job, family and such, reminding me for the nth time why I am still teaching.

Life is growth and change. Not only our body and appearance change over time but the face of life itself changes and has kept on evolving right from the dawn of human existence, regardless of how we picture the dawn. In the passing of eons, we progressed from living under the sky and in caves, cooking over open fires, to living in multiple room houses with kitchens and bathrooms, running water, electric lights and appliances, phones, and whole-house heating and air conditioning without even a second thought. Over the course of a little more than 100 years we have developed a communication system that allows instant discourse to take place between people, whether the recipient be in another part of a building, city, state, country or in outer space. In the age of electronics, the drum beat of hip hop and wrap, we are bombarded by so many influences, including scientific and technological progress, cultural and social change, and economic fluctuations, that our work load has not decreased, as originally thought it would. Since advances have made work physically easier and quicker, we fit so much more into the daily schedule.

A side effect of our advances is that we have come so far from our beginnings living in nature to our existence in a technologically oriented society that should we be lost in the woods on our own without recourse, we could easily be at peril, because we may be hard put to know how to survive. And because the distance from that original self and the culturally derived individual is often far apart, it is easy to lose track of inner needs and natural connection in favor of the culturally created ones as well. Indeed, many people have trouble seeing themselves as part of nature which to them, simply put, refers to the grass, trees and wild creatures out of doors. To be sure, we cannot ignore the culture in which we live, because it does, after all, seek to fulfill important needs of survival like making a living, having a family and interacting with the community of which we are a part and on which we depend. But in the modern course of events, we live a flashing-marquee existence, often, with only passing glimpses of unconscious needs, as there seems only time to react to the most obvious stimuli pressing us from the outside. With little time to sort it all out, we are caught up in latest trend, keeping up with friends, coworkers, living up to expectations of family and job, particularly during young adulthood. In essence, we live a two-fold existence in which the second part can easily sink into recesses of mind and soul. Often we are not aware something is going out of kilter, until a problem arises that we cannot resolve or we hit a kind of brick wall of not knowing where to go next, because we are so occupied with the immediate business and pressures of every-day life.

Seasons revolve around us, seamlessly, in the circle of time, as dependably as night follows day, as seasons hold positions of sun, moon, and stars, as certain as vernal and autumnal equinoxes. Many of us look forward to the changes of seasons that help us break the monotony of routine as surely as to special occasions like birthdays and anniversaries, holidays and vacations which we capture in albums and scrap books to languish over with family or friends or for our own enjoyment. These give us meaning and purpose and help celebrate sacred moments of being that contribute aspects of wholeness to our lives. Each season comes with a special personality of weather, occasions, fashion, and foods. Each season returns in altered ways, depending on atmospheric conditions, economic, political or personal circumstances, making each return different from the previous one. Each season presents a new beginning, sections in the book of the year, life revealed in new and unexpected ways, often despite best laid plans. Seasons are the framework for change in which we live, work, create, and play.

Seasons of the year pose an interesting metaphor for seasons of our lives. Often we equate them with age. But what about our own development and changing needs, creativity, and activities, can they not turn into seasons as well? As part of my course work in education, I studied the developmental stages of childhood and adolescence with fascination, focusing on learning tasks involved in these years of physical and mental growth. When I went on to teach adults, along with my own experiences in life, it became obvious that stages of development do not end in adolescence but continue on throughout adulthood as well. Growth can take place continually, whether it be through experience or schooling, physical activity or exercise, spiritual stimulation or creativity.

I have encountered no formal requirement of study involving stages of life relating to adult learners. From popular perspective, changes adults face in their lives through the years are rarely regarded as stages, nor are adult lives regarded as developing, except perhaps in a psychologist's office. But in the classroom of adults of diverse ages, particularly in writing classes, these stages are evident. Swiss psychologist Carl G. Jung, in the book *Aspects of the Masculine* in the chapter "Stages of Life," divides life, basically, into young adulthood and middle age, having set aside childhood and adolescence, primarily focusing on what he calls the second half of life, the missing link here. He points out that while children have the opportunity to go to school to prepare for adulthood, adults, regretfully, do not have such a guide to prepare them for the second half of life. But gradually we are beginning to notice the signposts left along the road of life, telling us a new approach is needed. In the twenty-first century, we have become aware that graduation from high school or college no longer signal the end of our studies on which we can ride for the rest of our lives. Due in great part to technological and scientific advances, we now have continuing education, first, to update work skills or help with careers changes or retraining and, secondly, to enrich personal lives, so that nontraditional students in colleges and universities have become commonplace. Other practices also acknowledge our changing life style and needs. Often these surface in community adult education or general interest groups, sometimes, also, age related, such as parent groups, retirement groups, dance groups, bible study and book groups, writers groups, art groups, and so on, addressing adult needs. Beginning with the mid-twentieth century, we have been faced with the task of dealing not only with rapidly progressing technological changes but with the task of aligning these with our own personal changing needs that fan out to increasing life expectancy.

I like to separate three stages in human development: the first encompasses childhood and adolescence, the second young adulthood, and the third middle age, the one many call the second half of life. That life takes us through seasons of develoment in the continuing cycle of "becoming" from marriage and family, job or career, empty nest, retirement, or second career and whatever else life offers, may seem a new concept for some. It may be unsettling to those who are set in automatic pilot. Yet each stage offers different opportunities and makes different demands, requiring some kind of conscious preparation, whether psychological, spiritual or educational. But contrary to our childhood and youth where we are culturally and officially channeled into attending school to learn basic skills, in adulthood the choice to build upon these skills is ours, unless it is a job requirement. Schools often use a catch-phrase, such as "educating life-long learners" and for good reason. Often adjustments to new skills and work place changes as well as technology related life style changes leave their effect on our psychological and spiritual outlook. But opportunity abounds, and we are free to choose in light of new awareness. Learning something new gives us more than a new skill; it can help us cope with changes psychologically and spiritually as well by allowing us to enter these new worlds as participants rather than recoil as arm chair observers or hold-outs.

Human development involves a functional body, flexible mind, and an engaged spirit. For these are in constant communication with one another, each an indispensable spoke in the wheel of life, each capable of growth right along. Change can be catalyst that becomes star to wish upon, freeing desire to set the compass for the quest to reach that once elusive goal, no matter what time of life. For "Hope deferred makes the heart sick, but a desire fulfilled is the tree of life," Proverbs, 13:12.

Seasons

What are seasons
        but a merry-go-round
        of days
to different times—

Seasons of Hope and Prayer

    Hope is prayer,
wish on a star,
spring's return of birds,
summer's sun,
fall's harvest moon,
winter's first snow.

The business of life unfolds
like leaves of a well-rooted plant
radiating in different directions.

We step into our roles,
chosen and assigned,
on the job and at home,
with family and friends,
and countless other commitments,
as into a change of clothes.

    We forget
where the real I resides
until prayer holds the course.

Our lives intersect
with those of others
like sea gulls swarming
crisscross in the air
as if directed by the Almighty baton.

There we glimpse in others
fragments of our lives
shining through the feathers
of another's flight.

    When we reflect
in waters of our being
prayer carries hope on its wings,
pulls together fragments
of our scattered lives.

When seasons change,
we often pause bewildered –
Why did it all have to end?

But loss and sadness
of leaving one season
soon fades into winds
and sunshine of the new.

    Prayer is hope,
return to the roots of the soul
in a walk in the park,
a letter to a friend.

    Prayer answered is
like the return of the egret in spring
in the ever revolving circle of seasons,
letting us move forward
each time as for the very first time.

Seasons of a River

Time
is a river
issuing forth
from the lake
its mother, counting
days and years
in stages of becoming
full measure,
infancy to adulthood.
The river runs
through landscape of what is,
current of energy its father,
nurturing life,
bearing goods of progress
by canoe or motor boat,
storm torn or peaceful
in sunshine or snowfall,
past bluffs of unknowing
and countryside of what is yet to come.
The river's course moves
through changing states,
which color its waters,
past borders of ordinary existence,
from teepee to log cabin to city.
Elements and human hand
change the river each season.
When life becomes too full,
river spreads to flood plain
transforms itself and life into new frontier.
Tributaries give strength, feed
renewed hope in another coming of age,
ever the same, ever changing.
The river travels its course
in bedrock of past
to gulf of present
driven by elements
and current of future.
It flows into the ocean of eternity.
Time is a river in the greater design.

The Override

        The power that overrides
        all other powers
        is so great

it imbues the tiniest seed
with all it needs
to grow to plant
to flower to fruit.
From deepest valley,
it raises highest mountain peaks
into sky.

When we temper
with one creature
of creation
or discover a cure,
we set off
an unforeseen chain reaction
of atoms we never
knew existed.

It is as though
tiny step by tiny step
we advance into the woods
without path.
We think we go in one direction
and come out at another.
Most times we cannot predict
where we will wind up.
Yet we cannot go back
from where we came,
because the seedlings
of our experiments
have changed the woods.

        The power that overrides
        all other powers
        also frees us to imagine
        what we cannot yet see.

Music of Ages

Different as movements
of Mozart's Symphony No. 36
each season brings a new beginning
in the concert hall of custom and fashion
on the stage of political trends

      Winter   adagio   allegro spiritoso
          January of the iron curtain
          brings the family to America
          to unfold a new adventure
          in snows of the Midwest
          Life starts over
          from the middle
          like when my son is born
          years later
          and I recognize in him parts
          of myself and my brothers
          so that I grow up
          once more with him

Spring   andante
      Trees gradually unfold leaves
      and I plant prayers
      colorful as pansies
      during my parents' Easter visit
      I resolve to my father
      to travel with the pen
      from now on
      through this country
      and the old
      he says he does not know
      what I was waiting for
      and I am reborn in May

      Summer   menuetto
          I submerge in arms of marriage
          as the world moves on
          the stock market rises
          then I find a house of all seasons
          on top of a hill

                near the lake of inspiration
                the one without fence
                where I can see the sky
                in any weather
                where seagulls and egrets
                chickadees and cardinals
                fly in and out

Fall presto
    Birds gather
    Children go back to school
    with *no child left behind*
    I go with them that I might learn
    from teaching
    what they need to know
    My daughter is born
    lively as tumbling leaves
    I learn to be a mother
    following her around
    because motherhood
    changes everything I used to know
    about family ties

Sequence of years does not matter
each cycle brings a lifetime of music
each season harmony changes
inspires new compositions
if I take time to listen

The Game Along the Way

Life is a participation game, a sort of Monopoly,
between you and me and the world,

played along the road of change,
on the train of vision,

across bridges of ingenuity,
and along paths lined with berries of good luck,

over mountains of challenge
and gullies of denial,

to the forest fire of disaster
and the spring of new life,

through valleys of doubt
and nights of mystery,

into the arms of love
and the dawn of truth,

into the daylight of understanding
and the orbit of transformation and growth.

Success does not follow the number of chips we hold
at the outset but on how we play the game,

on how far we have come and have yet to go
in the Easter of our tomorrows.

What My Father Told Me

Life is a canvas
and you fill it
with whatever you like

choose the colors and hues
the people and scenes

your picture can be
anything you want

you can create the world
in which you live

To the Muses

How subtle are your ways.
Sometimes you come, a stranger,
     opening the door into light.

Sometimes you appear a dove
     at the window of new growth.

Often you take me
     to the land of new visions.

Other times you enter
     an old friend into the day.

Together we walk
     down city streets of dailyness,
     along rivers of progress,
     through valleys of doubt,
     and mountains of hope,
     rest at the lake of reflections.

     Often overlooked in bygone days,
     enlightening, though, your visits were,

     your presence passed a babbling brook
     trickling into obscurity

     of an underground river
     that eventually reached flood stage.

     As events accelerate anew
     will life be rearranged by new floods?

     Or will the road lead inland
     to higher ground of acceptance?

You always return, and I assemble pieces
     of life's perceptions and events
     into wholeness of word and picture.
How subtle are your ways.

Circle of Renewal

On grounds of lawn
        where prairie grass once grew
        where traffic now rushes past
the maple stands tallest among trees
        fall branches still hold
        faded rust leaves

pines and spruce trees
        surround it prayerfully
the crab apple tree
        smallest among them
playfully carries cherry-sized fruit

each tree embraces
its own circle of life
        not grown from seed
        but from young trees
brought in and planted
        at the dawn of new vision

prairie grass has been restored
around lakeshore
        haven to wildlife

diversity of nature
        feeds and shelters birds
        and my soul
openness of a new landscape design
like the people
        that populate the land

Running for Life

The daily run starts
with sluggish mind, awkward limbs that long to stretch.
Pulse quickens with each step. I start way back at dawn
of humankind, jumping out of tree of exploration.
Running at a steady pace, the spirit hunts for the next meal
with first words that soon disappear into caves of ancient
visions and emerge languages scattering up Tower of Babel.

Speed soon propels me to the next eon on spiral road
of continuity in quest of Homer in the land of archetypal
exploits, home of the muses, companions of artists. There
Plato debates knowledge, forbidden fruit of another age
that blends into exploits of Beowulf. The course is now set
to Chaucer and his pilgrims, and I linger over their tales.

Pace slows over longing for *Paradise Lost*. Joining voices
of history, I leap across chasm of time, until we find ourselves
running through Shakespeare's dramas, as if they were mind's
marathon, strengthening muscle of our own lyric in trial run,
then stumbling over some quixotic attempts at intervals.

Soon I travel in a kind of automatic pilot, thoughts moving
through an unknown island of my existence like *Robinson
Crusoe*. The ship of imagination then takes us
to Goethe's *Suffering of the Young Werther*, across
mountains of faith to Rilke's reflections.

When we arrive in the land of Whitman's Song, we pass
from woods of unknowing into clearing of Dickinson's hope,
"the thing with feathers" flying from Freud's pond of secret
desires to Jung's city of collective unconscious. Breathless,
I rest, momentarily, on cliffs of life's river, near where
Indian Mounds look across to Cathedral and ponder
For Whom the Bell Tolls, when Woolf's perspective
directs my view anew.

Following footprints of the past, I submerge in the numbers
of the present. We can leave behind our own footprints
in rhythm of heartbeats on vellum, on paper or on the web.
New momentum reassembles fractured existence into one

picture. Our legs carry us further each time we run, wind of the past in our back. And every time we run, we outdistance ourselves.

Returning along the lake of inspiration feeling renewed and energized but tired, my pace slows as I arrive at the door of inception. Running with the seasons – I run for life.

The Larger World

Silence is refuge
        when life's carousel
        turns too swiftly

Silence extends the field
        through which I walk
        past wall of resistance
        from darkness
        into light of reflection
        revealing
        inner landscape if vision

Silence unites seasons
        past to present into future
        in an instant

Silence offers strength
        in a storm
        when words do not suffice
        when mountains touch horizon
        when I discover in the moment
        what I should have known
        all along

Silence is God's embrace

Skyline of the Faithful

Church steeples, houses of worship,
dot horizon on streets of Midwest America
like castles grace skyline
along the Rhine River in Germany.

Castles, fortresses of fairytale proportion,
stand occupied by owners of past glory,
reinvented, as museums or in ruins,
bearing silent witness to the past.

"On Milwaukee's East Side," my mother
once said, "you will find a church and a bar
on nearly every street corner."

"On Saint Paul's Summit Avenue," an observer
recently said, "you will find a church or two
and a college on nearly every block.

From Cathedral Hill to Mount Zion and on,
we don't know where to look first,
drawing the curious in as if steeple or shape
of building determined faith and affiliation.

Churches stand expanded, revived, converted,
world within world, to fill life's gaps beyond weekly
service and holiday celebrations, like Project Home
or Loaves and Fishes and other events and needs.

They carry on God's business, regardless
of ethnic preference or denomination, bearing
full witness to changing times. Churches
in the Midwest are fortresses of another kind.

Winding Road of Faith

The winding road of faith takes me
from childhood roots through what I cannot
see surround me nor what may lie ahead.

By day I travel blinded by the sun as if she were
mother to religion. Or I look for answers in clouds
of mythology as if divinity could be divided
into human traits. I discover God in a temple
of antiquity and follow the star to Bethlehem. I walk
the woods of intuition, descending steps of doubt
into a destiny ranging from sword of conversion
to faith in God.

I join those who travel landscape of life's experiment
like tourists. Life becomes a mansion, upon which
we happen on our way to somewhere else, a mansion
with too many rooms to count, rooms that attract
and confound, inspire and distract, part museum,
part living quarters, a Babel of sorts. We move through
them like through ages of history, from rite of baptism
to feudalism of allegiance and dark ages of fear
to renaissance of spirit, from enlightenment of belief
to industrialism and pragmatism of newfound knowledge,
past politics and wars of disorientation, to technology
of unending possibilities to times of reconciliation and love.
Having grown up once more in spirit of art and dance,
literature and music, we encounter new visions along
with mysteries untold. We recognize tradition here,
practice ritual there, only to arrive at politically correct
and scientifically sound. And the Keeper is seemingly
nowhere in sight to guide us past doubt and through
changes to the next step of the journey, unless we,
perchance, meet on the path around the lake or walk
through the park, away from the daily rush and hum.

Distanced from the Source by hype along the way,
I renew the flame midway, like a prodigal child,
conscious of the abiding Spirit within, in communion
with Creation, where roots of faith draw nourishment,
a seeker—in the kingdom unknown.

Sunday Service

People gather in pews, birthplace of poetry and writings.
Procession initiates anticipation.
Organ fills atmosphere, calling forth choral voices,
    lifts the spirit on angels' wings.
Tradition holds a steady course, while
Progress moves along a wavy line
    of what humanity presumes, assumes, hopefully
    carries forward through history, open-ended.
Reflection stirs belief without knowing
    the yet unknowable and leads to
Meditation of knowing only that the empirical alone
    leaves spheres of imagining even of that
    which is provable in empty vacuum
    above and below and without vision.
Sermon rescues from effects of static thought,
    impelling listener to examine and weigh,
    discard or annex that which is not easily
    put into words.
Communion shares the moment giving thanks
    under the dome of holy celebration
    for sun, moon and stars, rain and earth,
    and those who brought us here
    and those who will carry the relay forward
    in this world of our Creation.
Prayer moves along the time-worn aisle of worshippers' footprints,
    where saints and sinners meet
    the lost and lonely, rich and poor, the ordinary and grand.
    Need to connect brings them to join eons of the faithful
    from now until eternity.
Offertory intrudes the business of life, a la corporate model, call it
    philanthropy, charitable contribution, or giving what you can.
Praise for the Almighty holds up that which is holy,
    for we are all simply worshippers alike in His light.
Benediction calls on everyday life
    to embrace its circle like the first people
    east and west, north and south,
    sky and earth,
    in its center, the everlasting Creator of rolling spheres.

All Creatures Bright and Beautiful

      On the path
around this hill-top Minnesota lake,
where only sun measures time,
seagulls, geese, and heron's, at intervals,
claim tiny rocky island in its center.
Egrets fish along shoreline of lake
and nearby ponds. From reeds near path,
red-winged blackbirds give chase
to passers-by, past apple trees and aunt hills.
Pine trees stand sentry close to shore,
where deer bed down at night,
leaving tall grass thatched here and there.
Family of geese claims path down a way,
where blackberries grow plump
in late summer. I divert my walk
just as blue heron rises into sky, fading
into setting sun, draw in deep breaths
of renewal, reconnection. Here I am
but one in the chain of earth's beings,
in this Eden of all creatures great
and small, in worship
          that holds existence on its axis.

Timeless

Seasons fill pages
of years collected in this album
kept in mind's closet,
pages made up
of birthdays and graduations,
weddings and awards,
Mother's Day and Father's Day,
from Thanksgiving to Christmas,
Easter to Memorial Day
and vacation trips in all seasons.
Each picture imprinted on memory
life's celebrations as if days
in-between were behind-the-scenes
preparation, preserved like fossils,
sacred as a family's journey.

II. Spring, Source

I dwell in possibility—
　　　　Emily Dickinson

Every year we look forward to spring to be released from winter's grip. Spring with its longer days, sunshine and rain brings renewal and growth which gives us hope and new energy. Relieved of some of our layers of clothing, we feel closer to nature, while we spend more time outside. Spring is the time we may plan new projects, in a cleaning-the-house kind of approach to life. We may plan special outings, trips, or activities, because we cannot let precious daylight hours go to waste.

In terms of seasons of life, the most apt comparison of spring often relates to childhood and adolescence, the years of obvious physical and mental growth and development, the time in our lives when everything in the world is new. Life then is a constant chain of discovery and imagining, learning and dreaming. We move from awareness of our needs to recognizing parents and immediate environment to outside world. We learn to drink from a cup, tie our shoes, play with toys, interact with friends. In the process, we develop motor skills and mental capacity. The kind of behaviors children display, toys they choose can become early indicators not only of personality traits but of mental capacity and of future interests, hobbies, and eventual careers.

When my son was a toddler, he loved to play with match box cars and toy garages. One day, I found him alternately inserting in and removing two batteries from his toy ramp. I pointed out to him the ramp would not work without battery. His response: "I want to find out which battery does not work." Like many children, at various times he wanted to be fireman or policeman. At fourteen he owned his first car on which he worked so he could be ready at sixteen when he was allowed to drive it. His fascination with cars and with finding out how things work stuck with him into adulthood. Today he is a mechanical engineer specializing in design with a major Midwest company, and is frequently called upon to mentor others. In his spare time he refurbishes and shows antique cars.

Many childhood influences can be indicators of future vocational or recreational choices. As preschooler, I wanted to be a dancer. As young elementary school student, I took piano lessons and sang in the school choir. From the time my younger brothers were born when I was five and ten respectively, my activities also included them, since I increasingly was asked to help look after them. Eventually, I would line up neighborhood kids on the street to play school. I was always the teacher. By the time I finished grade school I had learned to love poetry and writing. But as the family went through a chain of relocations in difficult times, the last to America by ship, the library became my vehicle of imagination as I began to read my way through adventures in far-away places with Pearl Buck, Karl May, James Fennimore Cooper, Jack London, and Mark Twain, and others, as if this would prepare me for the real life adventure ahead. At the same time, faced with the need to prepare for a vocation, I dreamed of being a writer or fashion designer. But because of our uncertain circumstances, my desire to become a fashion designer, like the notion of being a writer, began to float in air; and the thought of ever attending a university, seemed as unreal as the stories of Karl May.

Yet most of these interests and desires found their place in my life eventually, like milestones, and they continue to do so. To my surprise and joy, I received a one-year college scholarship, undoubtedly arranged by my English teacher and high school principal, allowing me to graduate from high school at 17, and opening the door to my future. I saw myself through the remainder with work after school and a loan, completing a secondary education program with English and German literature from mythology to present. Thus, milestones, like college came about spontaneously, while my professional life was carefully planned, like teaching itself. Others arose out of necessity, like writing or emerged out of situations, like drawing; still others found their way into my recreational life, like music and dance.

An important part of being young is that we are allowed to dream, to imagine lives and occupations, perhaps try them on for size. We can imagine, beyond obstacles anyone or anything we want to be and where and how we want to live. We are free to do so in the privacy of thought or imagination, without penalty or real risk, fear of failure or financial concerns. But even failure can be part of our imaginings, part of trying on the mental shoe for fit. Perhaps the ability to dream is important in all stages of life, though it may become more difficult with time. In my case, I was born into a time of change, under the sign of Gemini, a fitting representation of my dual path of traditional and progressive roles played out in a conflicted existence.

What we, ultimately, choose as vocation or career, of course, depends on many factors. Influences in our environment and circumstances certainly determine both, opportunity and choice. Ability and talent and significant people in our lives channeling and encouraging, or discouraging, us, as well as work ethic, all have their influence. Educational exposure can become testing ground and beginning of a direction. Circumstances surrounding family, economics, community, politics, war, etc., all can have bearing, directly or indirectly, on career choices. A career choice is not always a direct line from interest to realization. And, in a world offering so many options, rapidly rising cost of education, and need for income, career choices become ever more difficult, so that many a career wish may turn into a job more than a calling.

But even if career and calling are one and the same, other interests, dreams, or desires may still exist, perhaps subconsciously or be relegated to second place, perhaps to a hobby, which is a safe alternative. Others may be deferred indefinitely or fall by the wayside because of lack of time, money, opportunity, or frequently, because of lack of practicability. Still, it helps to keep track of those original inspirations. Even if we have achieved our goal of working, ready to support ourselves and potentially a family, we are prepared for adulthood only for the time being. The belief that our education and growth are complete after finishing high school or college is outdated and misleading and can become problematic for some.

It is inspiring to follow sequences and turns in the life journeys of illustrious figures in history. What would have become of child prodigy, Wolfgang Amadeus Mozart, without his musician father? Frederick the Great, emperor and military strategist, was also composer, a little known fact, as he stood in his own shadow as ruler and that of Mozart's stature, along with other composers of the time. Benjamin Franklin was not only statesman and diplomat but scientist, author, and printer as well. Marie Curie became chemist and physicist, winning a Nobel prize, first jointly with her husband, then on her own, at a time when a woman's place was still relegated to the home. In more recent times, Maya Angelou began her career as performer only to become a new voice in literature. Czech born, Madeleine Albright, currently professor at Georgetown University, began a career in journalism and publishing but became Ambassador to the United Nations and the first woman to be Secretary of State of the United States. How many children dream of being president? Ronald Reagan began his career as popular movie star and wound up president of the United States. Barack Obama, after his work as community organizer and senator, moved on to become the first black president of the United States. Life is as predictable as it is unpredictable because of change that constantly unfolds.

Science tells us that in adulthood our cells renew themselves in continuous cycles to the end of life. We may not be aware that this is happening, and negative changes are often regarded as aging, when in reality they may be due to life style. How we take care of ourselves has a noticeable effect. It is safe to assume that with increasing life expectancy, this will play an increasingly important role in the future.

Since the spirit of spring can take hold any time during the year or during our lives, it may occur every time we feel inspired, every time we undertake something new. It is evident in the clichés of having "spring fever" and "feeling young again." An important part of that is being able to dream, imagine, envision that which we desire, the thing that could be, much the way we did in youth. As we mature, we have the advantage of bringing life experience and insight to new beginnings. It is never too late to learn something new, develop a talent, whether physical, intellectual or artistic, or to return to or resurrect an old dream to fill life with meaningful activities at any stage in life. After all, Anna Mary Robertson or, as she was known, "Grandma Moses," the painter, certainly did. It seems that flexibility in our thinking helps us not only adapt to change but lets us propel ourselves forward with our inspirations, no matter what they are.

Spring is Spirit, energy of renewal that gives us hope. Hope guides us to fields of new perspective, where faith leads us to new insight. Then the sun and rain of promise help us prepare for the harvest of our tomorrows. According to the Bible, "Those who till their land will have plenty of food," Proverbs, 12:11.

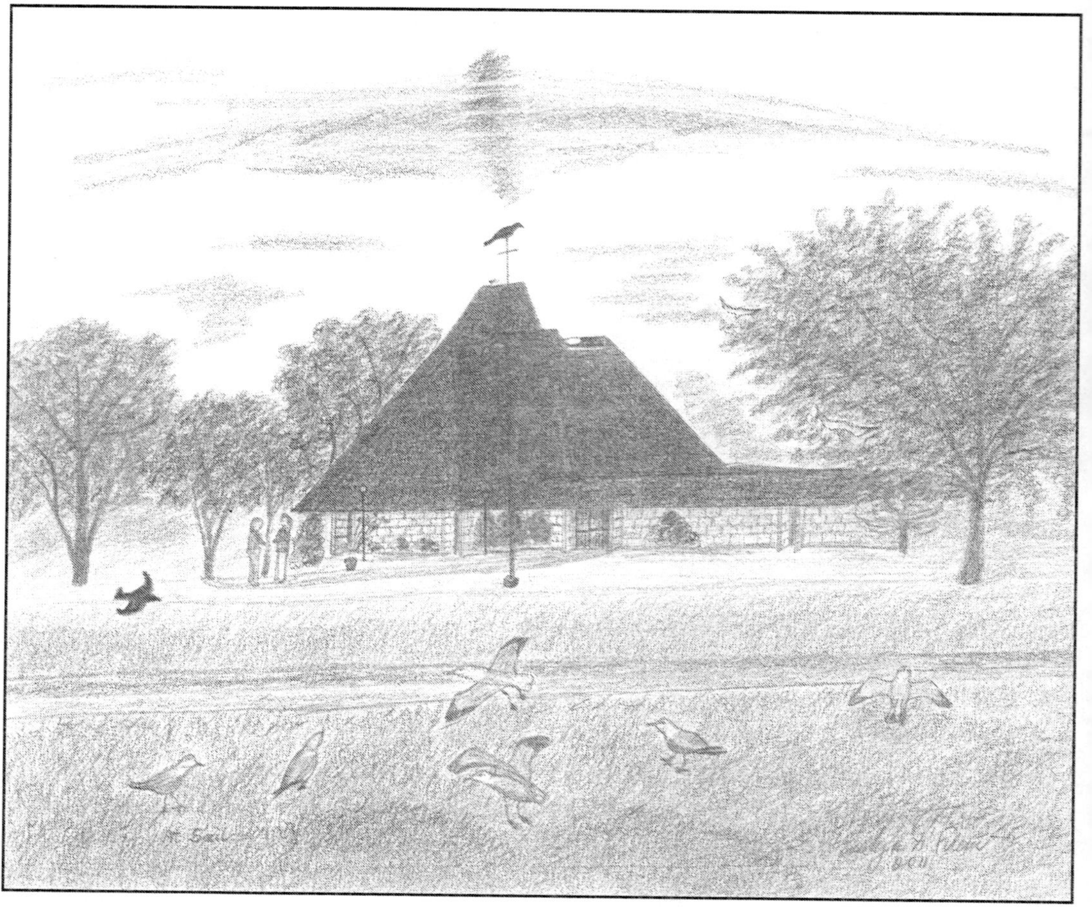

Awakening

On the lake
        emerald waves undulate
pulse of awakening season.

Inspiration

I drink your waters
to renew my spirit.

I come to you
worshipper bearing gifts,
praising your wisdom.

I pray
for sun to shine upon earth,
and rain to drench soil
that I may plant my seeds,
tend them,
watch them grow
into a plentiful garden.

Spring Winds

Wind-whipped snow waves
        that lapped winter's windows
recede into the earth
        leave the house
anchored in grass
        as though having returned
from some other-world journey

On the hill
        between sunset and lake
facing the city
        the house stands its ground
where prairie winds
        give new direction

The Melody

This morning
I awaken,
thoughts of you
entering my mind
like a favorite melody
flooding away
last night's gloom.

Maundy Thursday

In the eastern sky
golden moon
behind cloud veil
seeks to cry out
through silence

Lightening further east
crosses black sky
in uneven bursts
as if in voiceless sobs
of human sorrow

The Loss

       This year
the tiny African violet
does not drive blossoms.
Day by day
it fades
from the outside in,

       as if it were a candle
or a life
of someone beloved
just burned out,

       extinguishing
candle hours
of joy and gladness,
leaving only
open space
wanting to be filled.

Easter Meditation

      Easter morning the sun rises
      to the sound of organ and brass,
      bringing reassurance and joy

in aftermath of tsunami
that washed away so many lives in Japan,
we fear nuclear reactors hang in the balance;

in wake of tornadoes
that uprooted many families in the Midwest,
we recognize our own vulnerability.

And in the Middle East, where people
demand change and democracy,
we see familiar parts of a journey.

In the Midwest, where economic crisis
threatens ordinary existence,
teachers demonstrate for the right to unionize.

      Easter sun escapes
      prison of clouds today,
      seeding confidence and hope.

Easter surrounds fortress of faith
colorful crowds of worshippers seek,
ritual delivering us from a world of chaos.

Sun-warmed, we carry memorial
Easter lilies home
to grace communion meal with family.

We enjoy baskets filled
like memories of past seasons
in renewal of present family bonds.

Easter eggs of anticipation
lead to new direction
in meadows of hopes and wishes.

      In this ritual communion,
      we raise spirits, mingling voices,
      in halleluiah chorus of becoming.

The Wall and the Vision

The boat lay anchored in the harbor,
prepared to sail for the open sea
to fish in deeper waters.
But fog cast its net over harbor and sea—
Left me stranded to wade at the shore—
In the distance the foghorn blew.

Waiting for the fog to lift, I wandered inland
to the foot of the mountain slope
which lay draped in a curtain of grey—
A path rose before me obscurely,
but the fragrant forest invited me there,
when I heard the call of the hawk—

I went on, up the mountain
for a better view
and quickened my pace to the goal—
Mist, like a blanket,
closed tightly around me—
Still, I pushed on through the grey—

Against the pull of invisible forces,
my pace slowed; I gulped air—
and my destination seemed more distant that before—
Around me creation seemed a solid grey tomb,
a tomb built of great concrete walls—
when I heard the call of the hawk.

I pressed on, up the mountain,
inch by inch—straining to see—
Potent, unyielding forces loomed oppressively,
sought to entomb my ascent,
threatening to crush my being—
Still, I pushed on through the grey—

With remnants of vigor I faced the great block,
laboring forward – hope seemed lost—
Then a wall, suddenly, gave—
broke into large pieces, fell away—
fell into the great void below,
opening heaven above—

Red ball of fire glowed on the horizon,
bathed the heavens in red and bright orange,
burst at its fringe into sparkling yellow,
fused in the distance into blue light
light so brilliant, it blinded my eyes—
Yet I remained, ah—to gaze at the heavenly sight!

Below me dense fog,
above me no limits in any direction—
so vast was the resplendent expanse.
I deeply inhaled the crisp mountain air.
Feeling energy surge, I watched Aurora ascend
and silently move across the horizon.

Resurrection

April holds the whole year
        in one month
like humanity
        the seasons of life

April rain washes footprints
        from streets
bathes hope
        in fields of sunshine

April raises expectations
        for spring
then releases winter's last breath
        covering memories with snow

April is calm and storm
        of a troubled world
tornadoes uprooting life
        like war

April makes us want to travel
        the sometimes icy roads of change
through landscapes and sights
        of the unexpected

April lets us rebuild
        in the space of loss
in the neighborhood
        of innovation

Resurrection comes
        with thawing of lakes and rivers
budding of plants and trees
        return of hummingbirds

For all its changeability
        its diversity
April is the constant
in the remaking of life

The Egret's Return

When the egret returns
        to the pond in spring
        he catches the eye with delight

does that mean you will return

when he fishes along the shore
      day after day

does that mean you are thinking of me

perhaps it simply means
the egret has found a place to fish
      and life goes on

Promise

March sun gathers joy
in its rays,
releases them
in snowy brightness
to Beethoven's Ode to Joy
in the rising of Easter spirit
and Handel's Hallelujah Chorus.

Sun rays fill the present
with symphonies of all those
gone before,
scales of harmonies and discords
of their concerts
like parts of themselves
they passed down to us.
Our parents
released us into that continuity
and the timbre
that distinguishes us from others
that we may create our own music.
Our children
carry parts of ourselves
in the drum beat of their rhythm
into a distant tomorrow
to a melody yet to be written

March sun gathers joy
into the arms of new beginning
and reawakens us
from hibernation of daily grind
with Bach's Toccata and Fugue
that wants to carry us forward
beyond Unfinished Symphony.

Mississippi River

       Life force of the earth, Titan,
       enchanting with sun-dipped face,
       challenging in bleaker state,
       draws us close to fish for dreams,
       look for direction.

We watch the current,
pulse of boats and barges,
inviting us to join the journey,
escorted by trains along its banks.

       We follow contours of the at times
       mist-veiled body, curving south,
       past bluffs and caves into flatlands,
       joined by tributaries, a nymph dancing.

           We lay claim
           to the River's ground
           as if it were ours to own.

       River of our destiny rises, like Proteus,
       beyond daily bounds, unexpectedly,
       regularly, as if it were
       a natural disaster. It sweeps

over house and field, over nest and tree,
sweeps into its valley time and again,
driven by forces greater than the pool
of all human willpower combined.

Like children we watch the River
bursting in the distance. Neither
lock nor dam can tame it
nor labor or prayer levee it.

       Risen above its bed onto the plane
       glaciers endowed it, irrevocably,
       the river god never loses center,
       sweeps along the way rivers do,
       taking its path full measure.

Nature's Song

I am the eagle
that glides high between worlds
the deer that ambles in tall grass
the mole that burrows underground
the snail that carries her shell
I am trees and grass and flowers
dirt and rock and streams

    I turned to the Earth
    that gave me life
    to the Sun that gave me light
    to the Winds
    that soothed and shook my existence
    and to the replenishing rain

        Why is She suffering so?

    I followed a spring
    to an underground river
    whose waters still ran clear and cold
    whose song pulled me
    away from life's oil spills
    and their memorials
    away from the plastic of forgotten days
    in the cemetery of immortal bones
    to clean up the foam
    which made her ill

The river swept me back
to the beginning
where wind and water play
and gulls draw arches
from sky to cradling sea

Prayer

We give thanks
for yet another spring
with yet another face,
bringing us to yet another gathering.

Guide our manifold efforts, oh Lord,
that we may tend the soil
of endless possibilities
and spread the seeds of harmony and peace.

Let our church be a shelter
of understanding and tolerance
in the storm of events and change,
where we invite a diverse people
to find a place around the table,
sharing the Spirit's rich bounty and grace.

Amen.

Mother's Day Observation

It begins giving birth, holding, nursing, the child,
trust of new life, no matter what time of day, occasion,
state of affairs or mind or economy.

It is Thanksgiving and Christmas, new years, Lent
and Easter, and all the days in-between, events and pictures
gathered from albums of occasion and happenstance, bound
into one book. Mom set the scene, the mood. We revolved
around her. Otherwise, where would we have been?

Mother's Day is commandment of heart, celebration
for gift of life received and cradled, acknowledgment
of skills and lessons learned and taught – model to live by.
Without her pose, her cheer, her frown, how would we
have known where we were going?

Her eyes look back at me from the mirror
of my youthful hopes. I saw her in that familiar pose,
reading books, and she had me read to her when I was little,
with the same blue eyes with which my son,
too, now queries the world.

I see her in fingers of my right hand, fingers
replicating patterns I watched her stitch into fabric, letters
I saw her string across paper, fascinated – unspoken skills
transposing themselves into my sewing a wardrobe
of thoughts, then writing a life to read.

Strands of her appear in my days like ribbons she
braided into my hair as a child, like dinner table settings
at birthdays and other celebrations and a quick concern
for others, just like my daughter. She organized family
activities and household to reveal secrets of living.

One half of me comes from her, like her quiet nature,
part of the Gemini I am – but brought to a new time
and place. In some ways, I have become my mother.
What are my gifts but tokens, unless I share with my
children and the world parts of what she gave to me?

Sunshine and Spring Winds

      Longer days and sunshine
      budding trees and bird song
      spring winds carrying children's voices
      take us back to the beginning

We put away heavy clothes and boots
make room for spring's new wardrobe
that defines who we will become
new shoes and sandals taking us on paths
rain washed clean of last winter's sand and salt

A parting glance at clothes
we have not worn for years
but are still good
yet no longer fit
or serve the changing image

We release them
like memories
stations of past days
to someone else
glad for the new find

the clothes having brought us
to the close of another cycle
we are relieved at the lightened load
and feel freer to move ahead
gathering energy and momentum

Surveying what remains
we assess prospects for the future
and after the Easter meal
share stories of new visions
in the family circle of continuity

      Like trees beginning their annual cycle
      we become stronger each year
      Like children discovering life's diversity and range
      we move hope onto a new course

Gift of Friendship

    African violets are
like constant friends,
blooming any season.

    April is their month
of resurrection. They are gifts,
memorials of Greek gods, transcending

    time, distance, and divergence.
Buds rise in continuous cycle,
whorls of petals, single or double,

    smooth or furled or wispy at edges,
unfolding like bells or rosebuds,
always revealing the inner core.

    Blossoms hypnotize
from miniature to size of dollar coin,
from whitest white to deepest purple,

    single color to triple tone,
and everything in-between. They
draw us into their beauty like nymphs.

    Their leaves a shape or green,
distinct as you and I that we know
the individual without the blossom.

    They welcome attention
like bright light but no sun;
they crave water but no flood.

    And if there is no time
for transplanting, they multiply
and grow to overflowing.

    And when one is lost,
we remember and look for it
wherever violets are found.

    And when one blooms
after a long rest, it's like
reuniting with an old friend.

    But no matter how many
violets we have, there is always
room for more,

        each blossom the giver's image,
each new plant a newfound friend,
each exchange a friendship sealed.

    For African violets fill
in colorful ways
an empty window on the world.

Pentecost

Grey and white clouds
cumulate
in May sky.

    Wind blows
a roaming spirit,
whipping across grass,
across boundaries,
fences and houses,
communities and states,
between animals and humans
regardless of their languages
of origin, as if to remind us
we are but parts of the whole.

    Wind bends tree crowns
not warm and mild,
as May wind might
but hard and cold,
taking our breath,
if only momentarily,
as in contest of wills.

    Wind tosses us
against elements,
in destiny sometimes cut short
by forces gathering strength
into tornado or hurricane.
Yet, between wind bursts,
sun descends upon earth,
warms winter-weary limbs
with anticipation.

Earth's energy emanates
from the same source
that creates all.

Father's Day Perspective

   Dad never went for sentimentality
but preferred honest affection.
He never strayed into nostalgia
but, occasionally, cast a brief glimpse back into the past.
He lived in the present, an eye always toward the future.

   His gift, as he saw it, was our presence,
the family's gatherings—no matter how many generations—
at dinners, on walks, in conversations. He was Christmas
celebration and Easter spirit, always harbinger of spring.

   I find his tall, slim, dark haired figure in his artwork
that holds up walls of my home, my being. There I see his
image in people and events, power of black and white
and colored woodcuts, ethereality of portrait drawings.

   His spirit, at times, appears to linger over my shoulder
when I write or draw. "So you're working," he'd say,
passing through the room from some errand, releasing
creative energy that carries me forward.

   I see him in fingers of my left hand, his left hand
guiding knives across woodblocks. The probing of his green
eyes returns my gaze from blue eyes in the mirror now, where
my features and expressions become more like his every day.

   My thoughts of the world cannot supersede his,
nor can my pictures replace his on the wall. Mine
can only occupy remaining space, fill in with my attempts
emptiness left, for I live in my Father's world.

   He—father, teacher, mentor, friend—sent me to find
my own world until I recognized the gift of his. He bestowed
on me the second half of the Gemini I am—Twins—
that sometimes stand at odds with each other and tradition.

   So I study perspective, learn from it and travel seas
of creativity into future of my own discoveries through layers
of existence, beyond resistance and fear, doubt and uncertainty
and venture to carry his gift forward. Every day is Father's day.

Dedication

>for Dr. Margaret Odegard who led the way*

Like Ulysses, she followed knowledge like a star,
almost beyond the "bound of human thought."
She led the way for the following generation,
pushed some through the concrete wall of cannot
and confusion into the light of revelation,
past "The Watershed" and "industry already comatose,"
traveling a gravel road to thesis destination.

And did "the last duchess painted on the wall, looking
as if she were alive," wonder what the "Lady of Shalott"
really thought while she sat weaving that she felt
so weary all the time? Did they envision "The Second
Coming" in a later age, or *The Power and the Glory*
of a newer world? We could have escaped to *Fern Hill*
to be "young and easy" once again.

Yet we followed her "To the Lighthouse"
moving forward once more and, like Mrs. Dalloway,
we stood high on the staircase of our being,
reflecting on the party as a whole. And we
discovered the same "force that through the green fuse
drives the flower," also drives us to blossom
and to spread to new domains.

"Unknown Citizens," we are drawn into the field
wearing a suit made for the new stage
"to strive, to seek, to find, and not to yield."

Coming Home

>When the robin returns in spring
>to build her nest again in the shrub
>near the study window,
>new promise fills the air.

When my children come over
with that familiar hug and smile,
leave their shoes at the door,
and head for refrigerator
or cupboards,
it is as though they never left.

Then I cover dining room table
with my mother's old table cloth,
the one with the permanent stain.
My daughter brings out her grandmother's dishes,
not for the sake of appearances,
but to nurture memories of her
who taught us the art of family dinners.
My son lights the candles for the communion
about to take place. We sit down
with my children's friends
in sight of my father's woodcut
depicting Columbus sighting land.

We rediscover each other
while we serve the meal,
and lively accounts take us
through courses of our daily encounters
of job and health, politics and people,
the way my father would tell stories
at dinner when I was a child.

>When the robin returns in spring,
>life renews itself the way it does
>any time my children visit –
>and I am long home again.

The Robin

Robin,
with your song
you bring dawn
to my window,
pull me from
the night's sojourn.

    Yesterday a baby robin
    balanced precariously
    on impatiens
    like an orphan
    too tame to fly away.

Was it your nest
under the neighbor's eaves?

    Today it scurries
    at my front step
    in fluttery anticipation
    of its mother's treat.

Robin, with your song,
your bring dusk
to my door,
extricate me
from the daily run.

Picture of My Children

Every flower is a poem,
 unfolding phase and story,
bringing past to present,
 holding seeds of future.

And when you stand
 among red and pink roses
richly clustered on their stems,
 it's a composition

of a thousand elements
 and you.

Invitation

        Let us watch the sunset
in the sun room,
        windows lined with violets.
Let us watch the crimson sun
        light fires of inspiration,

        sit there in easy chairs,
shed the shoes of dailyness
        in the dusk
of workday thoughts.

Let us scan horizon,
        watching
birds of hope
        seeking sunset's edge.

Let darkness approach
        canvas of our dreams,
fresh as springtime,
        for tomorrow's new beginnings.

In the sun room,
        windows lined with violets,
let us watch the sunset
        on its diurnal journey
into night.

III. Summer, Fountain

I live my life in widening circles...

Rainer Maria Rilke

Temperament of spring settles into constancy of summer, freedom to step outside dressed just as we are. We frequent farmer's market, enjoy beauty of roses sitting on our patio till late, swim in lakes and rivers at a whim, walk in the park soaking up sunshine to last us through winter. Summer lets us be one with nature more than any other season.

We enjoy a similar kind of anticipation for turning eighteen, better yet, twenty-one. If there is a rite of passage, today it may be graduation from high school or college or, legally, our birthday. But it comes without ritual or ceremony or life-altering experience, as it does in puberty. The newly acquired right to vote gives us a sense of power, real or imagined. The summer of our lives can start abruptly without sense of arrival. It is more like crossing a bridge to a new life. Like fledglings, some return to the nest after their initial flight until they try their second wings or remain in refuge from unemployment. Without map or guidelines on how to navigate these changing waters we call our times, we only know we will do things differently from our parents. After all, even Carl Jung called life an experiment. We advance our independence, move into on-going changes, because youthful rebellion demands it, because we want to live our life style. Beginning the first full-time job after high school or college, some are eager to learn the ropes; others are amazed the road up is paved with hard work. We find our way into the work-day world, dismiss what went before as outdated and see things in new light, our light. Some learn to adapt, fit in; some climb the ladder; others carry on best they can, or head for the success of a lifetime. Some, like me, align with new movements for the sake of work, until the movement becomes our own, and we open its door into the future for others.

Having worked my way through college as office assistant, I became a teacher, teaching my way through a new age from dream into reality. Writing at first, became byproduct of teaching until it became who I was and what I taught, while drawing became an incidental sketch or illustration, until it became second nature. I learned from teaching others what schools and colleges don't teach, about my work, details about human nature and learning, about myth and reality, like about the system, about art, and about the notion and definition of success, and more. The century that brought us Civil Rights Movement, sexual revolution, women's liberation and gay rights, brought old traditions into question, if not upending them altogether. All of us integrate changes as they move over the horizon and into our lives in our own fashion, ranging from avoidance to continuing education to new opportunity. Many see work strictly as income, something apart from what they would like to do. For others lucky enough to follow a calling, work adds meaning to life and becomes self-image and public identity.

A place of our own helps establish independence as well as identity. It means different things to different people, depending on what they need and can afford, whether they rent, buy or build. For many, as it is for me, carving a space for my family and me in a corner of existence is all important. It is not just the place where we disappear after school or work. Most of us need a place where we accumulate the stuff of life, a shelter and sanctuary, where we recharge energies in daily chores, in circle of family or friends, and the chance to be part of the community of choice. It is our universe where we can flourish in our chosen design. Home can be composting site of our lives, nurturing ground of personality and identity. It is the most influential environment of growing children, branch to family, revelation to friends.

We heed nature's call to romance. In my case, I danced my way into marriage in the name of custom and tradition, but wondering about progress and latest trend. Sealed by ritual and promise, we enter the most challenging venture of life. How we live together varies, seems mysterious and can shift like the surface of the earth, given the diversity of personalities along with societal changes. When children enter the picture, we become stay-at-home or working parents, blended or adoptive families. Our activities and lives seek to balance load of home and work in a new order of sorts in this unrehearsed performance. We watch over and guide our children, while we grow up with them once more but from a new perspective from "Gingerbread Man" to *The Cat in the Hat*, from *The Hobbit* to *A Wrinkle in Time* to *Harry Potter* through the world's mischief and challenges. We follow them to choir and band concerts, take them to scouts and swimming lessons, help them get ready for prom—and college. In the new family setting, through structure, rotation of chores, encouragement and support, we hope to instill in our children the new roles, free of gender stereotypes. Based on ability to live independently by choice rather than prescription, we hope their natural talents will take them where they want to go in life. Family provides roots and soil of the personality which they carry into daily activities that help form their truths and beliefs and represent the spirit in which they interact with others.

Summer of existence finds us productive, dominated by many influences, internal and external, responsibilities, and activities channeling our lives. But this mix is not a set equation in an era where so much changed. For instance, as a stay-at-home mom when my children were little, I took every sewing, tailoring, lingerie class imaginable, making it possible to cut corners for a struggling young family and to keep myself challenged, sewing everything from curtains to winter coats. It allowed my husband to concentrate on his career, his passion. It allowed me to channel some of my artistic fervor, though I may not have seen it as such then. This lasted until the children were of school age, and the need for more sent me back to college, where I studied literature and discovered Virginia Woolf, and afterwards went back to teaching. The wish to learn, to expand, to keep moving forward, remains my star to wish upon.

For many like me, with family and work, life can overflow. But when I started out, family and job were main goals that would bring fulfillment and income and help see us through. We have no idea of where all of this leads, ultimately. Despite best hopes and plans, we do not know how far our careers or jobs will take us, how our marriages will evolve, nor where our children will go, once they become adults, nor what our lives will be like when they leave. Busy with demands of life, we, often, do not react to gradual changes approaching. Even as we feel twinges of some things not being as they might be, we may ignore them and surrender to the automatic pilot of daily activities on the carousel that Hemingway calls life.

Children growing up, early retirement, longer life expectancies, suddenly change the picture of reality. In education we talk about the period of infancy expanding into the late twenties. With longer life expectancy, it is consistent to see the productive middle years expanding as well. Perhaps we saw our parents go through the empty nest period, saw them retire and thrive. But those were our parents; and that was then. Some may want more, continue to be part of the mainstream. While opportunities of the past may have waned, life has opened up in other ways. Often ahead of his time, when my father retired from commercial art, he devoted himself fulltime to teaching and graphic art, while sharing household responsibilities with my mother. This freed her to devote time to her interests of reading, needle work, and socializing. Today, at midlife, many wonder about the things they wanted to do, about vanished dreams, about life passing them by.

The August of life may leave many productive years. Energy once used to rear children can be channeled into another generation of children—those of creativity, new career, the arts, volunteer project, coaching, travel, study. If we can think of it, we can probably do it. How energizing is the prospect not simply to wait to grow old or make lunch a career, if people can reinvent themselves? They can dream as they did as kids, but better. Versed in experience of living and working, they are more independent than when first leaving their parents' house. With change eroding original premises in the world, it seems reasonable to make changes in personal lives, aligning with the new Zeitgeist in a graduation of sorts into a new life stage.

In the second half of life, the journey tends to turn inward for spiritual meaning. According to Jung, many people run into trouble during this time, in part, because of their changing but unheeded needs. Anchoring too much in the past can also add problems. Church, meditation and prayer gradually find their way into people's lives. Another factor affecting our psychology is changing distribution of masculine and feminine hormones of each sex. Men and women, gradually, seem to trade roles, where men take a softer approach, while women become more assertive. This opens new possibilities for each in their on-going development. It allows people to take turns of who they truly are and what they are yet to become, like a stay-at-home mom becoming entrepreneur and business executive turning writer. The new stage is the perfect time to catch up on neglected or deferred dreams and desires. According to Matthew 6, "search, and you will find; knock, and the door will be opened for you."

For Hope

To the Sun

Lily pads rise
        from the pond
here and there
        in a snake dance
to the sun.

The Premise

The premise of our attraction
remains unchanged:

Like two separate rivers
we follow separate courses
until we converge
and flow as one.

Like two eagles,
gliding in current,
we share our private world
apart from all the rest
until we branch off again.

In Concert

Beneath blue skies
clusters of roses
crowd together
      choir of red
      in rhythm with the wind
that sends flourishes
of petals to the ground

      Between octaves of blossoms
      crescendos of new buds
           praise their Creator

Fourth of July

      Flags and fireworks,
hymns and hot dogs,
parades and people gathering,
celebrate the spirit
born of hardship and success
in the country claiming
independence and belonging,
world within world.

      Discovery of America
brought to the surface what should have been
self-evident right from the beginning
but was obscured through ages
of building structures upon structures,
world upon world.

      Like the first people but at another time,
they came to start over, by default or design,
on pristine soil of new beginning,
until only a hint of the past was left.
Immigrants turned pioneers, they followed
the sun of hope across the continent,
free at last by sweat of the brow,
planting seeds of a new country,
world into future.

      From native peoples to Pilgrims
and immigrants, from Colonies to States,
the trail coursed west over hills and valleys,
over mountains and past canyons,
through deserts and down rivers,
through storms and in sunshine,
until tracks crisscrossed the land.

      The Dream keeps wanting to expand
just as masses keep coming.
They trek the course, discover and examine
for themselves these "self-evident" truths
and "certain unalienable Rights,"
labored plantings of past seasons
as diverse as the people themselves,
world without end.

Summer

turns
the rest of the year
into sets of superimposed
pictures of scenes and
faces that blend into
yellows and greens
blues and reds leaving
only a few personal
snapshots of special
occasions and summer a
full roll of film

Riding out the Storm at Orchestra Hall

    From the West, fluffy white clouds
move over Peavy Plaza, crowding
into deepest gray, wind tearing
at my napkin. The stage is set.

    Inside, Beethoven's 7th Symphony
first gathers chords slowly, then playfully,
only to slow down again, rocking us while
unleashing the movement. Second movement
sends forth flying staccatos and turbulent tympani
as in a hymn to the Almighty –
rain pelting windows and pavement, running off
in rivulets at the curb – The soul turns over
and over. The conductor, having lost the score
to soul's storm, pulls musical tones
out of the orchestra, sheer energy of his hands –
A tornado was sighted at 26th and Hennepin –
The last movement has horns blow in rapid bursts,
driving strings to follow thundering rhythm,
rearranging the soul yet again. Musical tones,
rhythmic runs fill the senses, filter into my bones
in a dismantling of expectations. I close my eyes,
staying clear of windows, per warning, yielding
to the power of this musical storm. Ah!! Breath
expels into roar of applause inflating the hall.

    Then I am released to silence
of open road, lightening-streaked sky. Rhythm
of rain on car windows and road overtakes
sounds of symphony resonating through
my being, an echo fading, absorbed by glare
of street lights on wet pavement.

The Other Half

     Life starts over
halfway through adulthood,
when the children leave home –
the marriage is over –
end of a dream.

It's like moving to another country:
customs are different,
and you have to learn
to fit in all over again
in the new role – mid-life single.

To fill the space,
you pick up the other half
of the dream you neglected,
the half you thought
had slipped away.

You throw yourself into action
that becomes force of a new spring.
Because fifty is the new forty,
forty the new thirty and twenty – Well,
they say the age of majority is rising,
where adults dress and act like the young
to grow up who knows when
in the age of increasing life span.

Teacher becomes artist;
laborer becomes entrepreneur;
doctor becomes journalist;
engineer becomes photographer;
and poet turns dancer
in the ballroom of the new age.

     So you can reinvent yourself
in the second half of life
for a chance to catch up
and dance all the dances
you never danced before.

The Empty House

Out of the blur of houses,
this one seems to promise, like the first car,
the move to independence,
passport to new beginnings.

From the recessed front door,
the "Oh!" of living space greets
with high-slanted ceiling leading to skylight
that lights the room like a chandelier,
enough to inspire an artist. Wood-framed fire place
uplifts the eye right back to passing clouds above.
White washed walls are like pages on which stories
of new experiences want to be written, canvas
on which pictures of new visions beg to be drawn.
This newness seeks identity, freedom
to grow into and expand beyond its walls,
like the young trees and shrubs outside.

Facing west, the sun room, entered through glass doors
like through a memory from long ago, is made
with a window wall, perfect for African violet plants.
At right angles, the bedroom is large enough
to hold even the most elusive dreams that can take shape
in the potential study overlooking the lake of possibilities
at the other end of the house, near the bright kitchen
that offers room for new creations, the remaking
of old family traditions with a sprinkling of surprise,
perhaps even accommodate the old sewing machine
so used to stitching together pieces of living.

In the dream, I see familiar furnishings arranged,
making the house look already occupied—Time has come
to move. Here sun, moon and stars will set the course.

Two Green Apples

    Along the path
by Markgrafs Lake

        an egret and a heron on their island
see us invade their peace
just then the heron takes wings west

    along the path
by Markgrafs Lake

        two trees tempt us with golden apples
that come down green
like friendship not yet ripe

        you cradle them in your big hand
blemished and imperfect
like our lives
yet pure in substance
one for you and one for me

        two green apples
part and come together

        time and again
mark fading days of summer
while turning harvest gold

    Along the path
by Markgrafs Lake

        egrets feed and geese converge
till apple trees bear red-cheeked fruit
two for you and two for me
we carry them as if in trust
like friendship colored love

Mississippi River Bend

No barges here
where the river bends
bordered by trees
like a lake in the country
yet linking two cities

    we sit at the picnic table
    reading the river
    as if from two different books

cloud formation frames
sun that placed a path
across the river
to the other shore

to its right and left
sun beams dance in current
extinguish falling like fireworks

    our thoughts disburse
    lost in river's steady current
    toward the Gulf

    we travel along
    for hope and joy
    you with what you call
    a vagabond sun
    I on the sun path
    to the other shore

then dusk extinguishes
river's fireworks
shadows swallow sun
a father calls his children
cool wind rustles trees

    we are left with sun
    that warms from within
    and return to the capsule
    of separate lives

Shooting Stars

in the summer sky
are for young dreamers

> twentieth century minstrel
> says she does not know fame
>
> her shaved head uncovers
> beauty of truth
> shape of her conviction
>
> into the microphone
> she sobs pained childhood
> memories of home
>
> beneath long lashes
> languid eyes do not flinch
> because the terror of childbirth
> has nothing to do with marriage
>
> It does not hurt
> to share pain and longing
> hidden beneath
> t-shirt and loose clown overalls
>
> the stage frees her into being
> in working boots of womanhood
> it only hurts not to share
> what the older woman
> did not want to hear

The young flock to concerts
for her stories
and their own

Shooting stars
in summer sky
are for dreamers
who know where to look

Athens Olympics 2004

   Olympic Summer Games unfold,
tribute to ancient gods and modern spirit
celebration and triumph
of human body and mind,
under flame of striving
   in brotherhood of peace.

   Persistence challenges endurance;
strength partners with stamina.
Imagination directs performance
in the choreography of dreams,
each generation seeking
to surpass the one gone before,
regardless of race or creed,
national origin or gender
in the race to be first.
Inside the expanding arena of sports,
athletes and standards,
   dreams turn into possibilities.

   They push beyond
established borders
for the privilege of participation
or recognition of their representation
in wind and dust of these ancient games
in the sun of friendly competition.
With cries of victory,
tears of joy and sadness,
they reach new highs
on soil of equality
   surrounded by colors of their flags.

   In this haven they are united
in language of body and spirit,
global village of progress,
against conflicts of ages.
Success of one elevates all in the race
of Games around the globe to reunite
from spring of antiquity to river of modernity
and all places in-between,
   in light of the common goal.

Four in One

    Worship follows
heavenly signs on the journey

Meditation

    Generations have passed
through these portals of Hope
on footprints of the collective spirit,
seeking Light of who we are
and where our journey will take us.
Worship is devotion more encompassing
than boundaries of any one language.
"When We Are in Deepest Need,"
the organ lifts us from within,
and when the sermon comes
wind of prevailing season, it rearranges
our notions and beliefs on the altar
of faith and reality. We respond
with hymns of praise, making room
for body and spirit to reconnect. Light
streams through stained glass, a mosaic
of prayers that bring us in communion
with the colors of our being. Assuaged,
we feel transposed into His presence.
Only human we become new creations –
"All things bright and beautiful."

Creation

    Worship unfolds a walk in nature
that holds the world on its axis. Away
from the fog of the daily schedule,
only the sun measures time. A walk
opens the soul to creation of which I am
but one of its beings, and I submerge
into my surroundings like the muskrat
diving below the bridge. Here wind
brushes face like a spirit, and I become
the child looking for a fort among trees
by the pond, the adult feeding ducks

and geese on the shore. Scents
of deciduous trees and grass fill lungs
in a deep breath that I hold
when the egret rises before me, slowly
unfolding wings like a cathedral ceiling,
then rising and fading above tree tops
into distant setting sun—
      "All creatures great and small"

Communion

      The dinner table invites worship
when every chair is filled
in the sharing of the meal,
in the gathering of generations,
where every hope and happening finds
a place at the table
in answer to untold prayers.
The exchange of stories nourishes
like the food we pass around the table,
from working life to pastimes,
hopes and fears, disappointments
and successes in the search for belonging,
equalizers of human existence.
When we open the wine of hospitality
against the scene of economic hardship
space shuttles and missiles, talk of war
and people facing red light of poverty,
we nourish the spirit with hope.
We break across borders of Babel
into universal language of communion
that opens the world anew in one Spirit –
      "All things wise and wonderful"

Grace

      Family Sundays worship creation,
all the parts of who we are gathered
into one whole, trees and seedlings
in the garden of the inner world,
in the house where we grew up.
Open doors invite renewal in the refuge

of unconditional love between generations.
And the building of community
depends on learning its ways to follow
our calling of work, productivity,
and giving that it may grow and thrive
in the circle of hospitality, neighbor
to neighbor, like an extended family.
Then we are prepared to move
into the larger world, global village
of new consciousness, to forge human bond,
because we are part of the earth, of all creation.
The landscape of our lives reflects in languages
we speak. Exposure to, immersion in them
lets us expand our thinking into life's diversity,
to understand what it means be fully human
in the mystery of what the kingdom has to offer.
"The Lord God made them all"

Worship brings us back
to the center of who we are
in body and spirit of God's Creation.

The Painter

        He claims possession of walls,
silent witness to days and nights
embracing my existence,
the way only a contractor can.

Furniture regaled to the room's center
I float around a lingering spirit
on a construction site.

        Mounds of sheet-covered possessions
landscape rooms lined with tarps
at their borders, inviting pails and painting
paraphernalia that take on lives of their own.
With spatula and cutting tool, he prepares,
sets about his tasks, a surgeon at work.

        He opens a new chapter of this house.
Rolling paint onto walls, he erases the past,
opens new pages, where interplay of darkness
and light determine shade and hue of color.

How will the scenery change
from windows of African violets
to skylight of visions,
from bookshelves of past journeys,
spaces for writing, creating, and teaching
to table of sociability and communion,
bedroom of nightly odysseys,
kitchen of rebirth, and bath of renewal
in the next chapter of the journey?

        He strokes on coats of paint
sorcerer transforming light,
lover working with care,
artist taking pride.

        He will return the walls to me
when they glow.

Fresh Paint

      Fresh paint erases the past
from consciousness,
turns a new page,
in shades of living,
launching pad for the future.

      "It's like a new house again,"
the carpenter says.
"It's just like moving," I respond,
surveying piles of clothes like a life
waiting to be sorted. It is a field trip
reacquainting me with things active
or forgotten, people slipped out of my life,
events long overtaken. Some are readmitted
into the storehouse of memories;
others are released to the world;
still others are simply discarded. It all leaves
me anxious to create new pictures
of rooms in the new universe.

      Even entry doors await their coat
of oil paint, after some hesitation.
Because it matters where
the doors lead in this launch reinventing
existence, and because it matters who
steps over the doorstep into my days.

Apollo and the Artist

    Apollo lights the truth,
invites the artist to move between
cumulous clouds and into the sun.
The artist exists somewhere east
of the rainbow, near the river of life.

    There I spend my days
in company of Muses, searching
along cliffs of truth for caves
of understanding on river banks
where Muses find their inspiration.

    I first came because my father sent me;
then my mother cheered the journey;
and the children inspire me to go on.

    Muses surround me in circle
of their dance. They laugh with me
and cry with me. They sing to me
while Orpheus plays the lyre.

    Muses watch me ponder
constellations of stars as I piece together
stories of resurrected yesterdays.

    I write for them and read to them
or draw pictures of the universe,
while distantly, Apollo lights the vision.

    When I should chance to go off
somewhere on daily errands,
Muses follow me.

    When I leave clouds,
on mundane business, they look for me
as if I were lost. Together, we return

    to shores where they reside, my home,
which now lies anywhere
their gentle spirit roams.

Pilgrimage to Lake Michigan

What is a dream
        but a Great Lake
too deep to see bottom
        or other shore
an inland ocean of wishes

like childhood
        where today is all
we see and hear
        and tomorrow is
everything we imagine

waves dance
        shades of green and grey
and purplish blue
        collapse and crash
like thoughts
        against retaining blocks
in their foamy reach
        for the shore

as if the dream wants to be
        dreamed over and over
into adulthood
        each time
a little different
        past aroma of bread and beer
past containment of self
        at the foot
of a city's heart beat

seagulls sweep water's edge
        hover and dart for the catch
feed our dream
        that moves inland
more each year
        and craves renewing

we know we must return
        to the lake
mark our place and look for signs
        each season of life
and generation of desire

Song of America

> In Memory of 911
> (Including lines of "The Star-Spangled Banner"
> and other patriotic songs.)

O say can you see . . .

This land is my land
    where I gave my children life
    in the home of untold possibilities.

This land is your land
    refuge in the storm of global
    conflict and intolerance,

From California to the New York Islands,
    where people weave the tapestry of their diversity
    connecting points East and West, North and South.

This land is made for you and me
    to live the religion of our hope,
    color of our spirit, energy of our work.

O beautiful for spacious skies,
    New York towers, gateway to America,
    harbor to the world.

America! America! God shed His grace on thee
    in that collision of darkness into light
    from strength of steel to eternity of dust.

And crown thy good with brotherhood,
    where helping hands in time of need
    turn the wheel of fortune of community.

From sea to shining sea
    They came looking for a new life, for land
    adventures, and riches and found home.
    They built roads to the future,
    bridges to connect the past, leaving
    landmarks for generations to trace.

My country, 'tis of thee
>our spirit is made, vast in its expanse of hope,
>starting life over as if they were
>the first man and woman.
>
>They move inland, across country
>like on the Oregon Trail,
>listening to lone wind over prairie,
>watching bald eagles fly at the Mississippi,
>catching sight of deer in forests of survival,
>nourishing on fruits in the valley of life,
>until they reached the Rockies of success.
>They traveled through deserts of endurance
>and blizzards of uncertainty,
>breaking ice of old traditions.
>They traversed canyons of imagination,
>entered woods of new encounters,
>moving on to lakes of abundance.
>They navigated rivers of their lives
>to fertile shores of invention,
>growing cities like cornfields.
>
>Now we climb mountains to technology,
>to the future in the stars,
>and to the human cause,
>part of the Global village.
>In common aspiration,
>they, who now are we,
>the country, bonded in United States.

Sweet land of liberty,
>where life is what we make it,
>in country, city, home or workplace,

Of thee I sing,
>seeding dreams like wishes
>in our forward moving lives.

Land where my fathers died
>planting roots of democratic ways
>for the ages of children yet unborn,

Let freedom ring
>from Atlantic to Pacific, borders North and South,
>and all other parts that constitute the Whole.

And the star-spangled banner in triumph shall wave
>over the founding dream, unfolding, expanding –
>carried forward in eternal colors

O'er the land of the free and the home of the brave,
>to have and to hold,
>each day like the first.

I'm proud to be an American.

Well Rooted

When days are
        like the rose bush
that brings forth
        so many blossoms,
clusters that, like heads,
        bow on stems
nearly to the ground,
        it is
as if in homage
        to a greater Spirit.

Between bent stems
        new shoots appear,
candle-like buds
        reaching straight
for the sky.
        They unfold undeterred
by storm or pelting rain,
        drawing
their energy
        from that same Source.

The Vortex

A walk around the lake
is worth a poem.

     I ground with scent of water
and grass along its shore,
connect with sound of gold finch darting
back and forth between thicket and open space.
Calls of sea gulls above water hint
summer is on the downward spiral,
draw me into the vortex
of this revolving universe,
wind whistling through my hair.
Evening sun throws its carpet
of reddish gold west to east
across the lake
     where an egret ascends,

carrying my thoughts with Him
into diminishing point of graying sky.

Phoenix Phenomenon

Struck by lightening

        the forest burns

Purified

        it starts over

IV. Autumn, Gathering

*That which humankind does not know
or does not consider
flows through the heart's labyrinth
during the night.*

Johann Wolfgang von Goethe

Autumn arrives, and we retreat into the ark of transition, preparing for winter's sea. Amidst bursts of fall colors, ducks and geese gather on water, while sea gulls circle overhead, ready for migration. Farmers bring in last of the harvest. People flock back to fiscal rearrangement of their seasons. Closets yield sweaters, jackets and solid shoes for fall's new look and feel. Energy zapped by hot summer days returns.

Fall's energy offers new beginnings that often change lives at home, school, work, or play. From the day we first enter the world we build the pyramid of our experiences. On my daughter's first day of kindergarten, I took the proverbial first-day-of-school picture, wondering how she would fare in the new, more structured environment. But in her usual out-going, lively manner, she was excited to join the other kids on the school bus that stopped in front of our door, easing somewhat the lump that began to form in my throat. By lunch time she returned home and delivered her enthusiastic report of her day.

Nowhere is the upbeat of fall activity felt more than in schools. Despite what some imagine, most young students are eager to return to school, bored with games of summer, wanting to reconnect with friends and classmates they have not seen all summer and ready for the next grade. Many adults sign up, at last, for courses or degrees they always wanted to take or complete. Teachers put new ideas into practice, give bulletin boards a fresh face, perhaps teach a recently created course, and see what has changed among students and colleagues. Fall's purposefulness and creativity surpass spring, when things wind down toward summer. Autumn is popular kick-off season for all sorts of other activities as well, including new model year cars and appliances, books and clubs, etc., and, of course, football. Those not included in the season's dynamics may feel left behind, unless they pursue their own activities. No wonder elections are held in fall. But it does not really matter so much what we do or return to but that we join the community as it comes together again in purposeful pursuit. Many people like to contribute, give back, whether they get paid for it or not for that sense of participation, belonging, and self-worth, benefiting participant as well as community.

When we first enter a chosen job, field or career, we discover, we are initially there in training, as in industry, getting to know company and products. In teaching it takes two years, to get the basics of teaching established, five years to polish and expand course content, after which it's time to start over. The dynamics of no two classes and no two school years are alike. Change is the constant here.

Perhaps it took outsourcing of jobs that sent along with them the skills of "made in America" to realize the importance of active participation in the work force. It seems reasonable to assume high unemployment is linked to jobs that are no longer available. Ageism is another way people lose participation through the lure of early retirement by excluding people who still have the ability, experience and expertise to contribute. We have somehow convinced people beginning in their forties, barely halfway through today's life expectancy, that they need to defer to younger job seekers. These are all factors that have more to do with economics of a nation than the reality of people's abilities, productivity, and needs. Obviously, these issues are complex and require time to be fully understood and worked out. It does have its psychological effect, however, on those involved, particularly with on-going technological changes eroding their tracks, so that they question their own ability and self-worth. The lucky ones go back to school, find new directions, reinvent their lives. It is adaptability that lets us survive hard times.

But many people look forward to retirement, often because it offers new possibilities. When my father, Wolfgang Klein, retired the first time at age sixty-five, he was happy to leave behind a job of commercial art. But retirement was short-lived, because he always considered graphic art his actual profession. For him to continue his work on art was as natural to us as his being our father. Soon he, also, returned part time, to teaching art, which he had done earlier in life and wrote his book, *Basics in the Visual Arts*. At seventy-five he retired from teaching. He continued work on his woodcuts, giving one-man art shows, as he had throughout his life. His intellectual capacity to keep up with and anticipate developments, including in politics, current events, environment, and any other issues of importance rivaled that of a young man and remained constant throughout his life. He continued his artwork until he was ninety. As artist-in-residence my father was well known and respected in Wisconsin and other places.

Retirement was a period of peace and contentment for my parents, despite empty nest. My mother benefited from the fact that after retirement, my father volunteered to prepare the meals, freeing her to pursue her interests. Further, my parents traveled for weeks on end in the United States and Canada, my father usually returning with sketches he turned into powerful woodcuts.

My parents were blessed with a long and happy marriage and four children, each of whom they encouraged into professional careers. My father's insight and creative approach to go beyond convention and tradition account for his success as husband, father, teacher, mentor, and artist. That, along with my mother's support, allowed us to travel further as adults than we may have otherwise. When I was a child, he told me girls can be successful at anything boys are, if they so choose. He, also, showed a young male friend after he had his first child, how to care for the toddler at an age when men did not do such things. My parents did what Joseph Campbell called "following your bliss." For my father it meant being married to my mother and creating woodcuts. For my mother it meant being married to my father and living in a comfortable home. They were the perfect complement for each other.

But not everyone is so fortunate. For some of us it takes longer to find our way, as many of us may not know where to look in life's many, often enigmatic directions. Jungian psychology tells us that there is a part of us we do not know that appears to have a life of its own in our subconscious. Frequently, it remains deeply embedded in the psyche for various reasons. For instance, my father, recognized the writer in me long before I did. I cannot help but wonder how much more he realized about me. Yet it was not until after his death that I discovered while writing my second book that there was a visual artist in me waiting to be released as well. Since I had a clear vision of what I wanted for the book, I had no choice but to launch my humble beginning. Visual art has added another dimension to my life; it was a missing link. Sometimes, it is only when challenges become more pressing than the influences that hold us captive and we are without recourse that we come through the fog to the door and step into a new life.

With so much happening in the world, it is the lucky ones who can follow their bliss right from the beginning, like the football hero who rises from high school sport to college to pro; or the child actor who becomes adult star; the computer wiz kid who becomes adult millionaire; the marriage that endures and thrives a life time. But it is never too late to dream and hope, to strive, learn something new, travel, volunteer and let desire continue the journey under a new banner.

On this journey, meditation can bring about spiritual experience, the divine. It is one way to center, get in touch with the inner self, rediscover or reconnect with the core, the soul. There are many ways we can do this. It can involve, simply, a walk in the park, an evening of ballroom dancing. It can revolve around appreciating art or creating it. It can mean reading a book or writing one. It can be attending a concert or singing in the choir. It can center around theater or church, having people over for dinner and conversation. It can be travel and vacation. Perhaps a variety of these is a good choice. It all depends on what works best for us. Sometimes, a more structured approach is called for. Some people like to meditate in Buddhist tradition. I like western meditation and usually begin with the Lord's Prayer. I, then, focus on a chosen mantra. After fifteen or twenty minutes of meditation (no falling asleep) I close with another prayer, including, also, a prayer for someone in particular need of support. There are, also, other prayers or passages from literature and the Bible, such as Psalms and Beatitudes in Matthew and others that can serve to introduce and conclude meditation, depending on need. The important thing is to meditate, for meditation is repose on the meadow of being, in shade of the tree of life, under the sun of Creation.

Fall is the time we move activities inside, just as we turn, increasingly, to the inner self over the years. The flame burning within shines light into the soul that let's us start out new again. And we ask in the Lord's Prayer: "Give us this day our daily bread."

At Anchor

Autumn

Geese and ducks
        descend onto lake,
rise again, streamers into sky,
        at-dawn rehearsal
of their migration south.

River Routes

Saint Paul's Ordway lies anchored
a boat reflecting in waters
of weekend musical excursions.

On board, passengers glimpse a last view
of city and lights from behind colossal
windows. Inside the hull, scenery
changes as this vessel navigates in concert
with Muses through time and locale,
conducted in rhythm of current in Apollo's
setting sun. Overtures of river voices
pass by symphony of river traffic,
in setting of shoreline scenes.
On these journeys, we travel
as on an Odyssey, through states and lands
of imagination. We visit *Don Giovanni*,
and ponder over *Dr. Faustus*, linger
in *Four Seasons*, move on to *Brandenburg
Concerto*, and find *Mother Goose*
around the bend, revel in Folk Scenes,
and wind back to *Appalachian Spring*.
On return, passengers stand to applaud
for a journey well done.

We disembark in Artemis's presence,
reflection of *Moonlight Sonata*
and disperse in our cars like fireflies.
Trailed by musical notes, some of us
travel from port of music along shores
of the city's river back into our daily lives.

Scent of Leaves

seagulls
                stroke
over Battle Creek Pond
as if it were   the ocean
playfully loop the sky
crisscross

        breath
        of a new season

geese
                gather
on the feather-littered meadow
each side   of the path
walk in rows
like children on a rope

ducks
                disseminate
slowly
on the pond
like the people hiking
in pairs
or alone

Jazz Dreams

Smoke-filled room,
breath of beer or wine,
we dance cheek to cheek
to slow rhythm,
lyrics of love found and lost.
Holding close,
we dance the night away
in New Orleans' French Quarter.

Cigarette smoke gone now,
the singer says she did not
make American Idol, but
she is not bitter and carries
the tune on wings
of piano fingers, soft voice—
and CDs
at Saint Paul's College Club.

She sings the dream
that wants to wake
sleeping reverie of jazz beat.
Tapping feet desire
to dance on air ballroom steps,
cheek to cheek,
in flashback into night
of a near-forgotten time.

October Mums

      October mums
radiate sunshine
      with blossoms of amber and orange
yellow and pink
      reminiscent of Mom's smile
radiating from a frame of blond curls
      holding bright eyes
and a hundred secrets

      brisk winds leave them
cold but beautiful
      fragrant but strong
facing the season
      in a birthday flourish

      of Indian summer days
with more blossoms
      and warmth than expected
sending us toward winter
      with energy and promise

Transition

      October winds cross land
brisk and cold,
warmth of summer
a lover's half-forgotten memory.

      Geese fill air
in upbeat bands of sound and motion,
settling on Markgrafs Lake
in peaceful reassembly.

      Winds scatter golden leaves
across meadow to pumpkin patch,
past burning bush
to wall of corn field.

      Autumn moves forward
now mild and sunny,
then cold and harsh,
roses and geraniums still blooming.

      Autumn does not hold back
like someone afraid to speak
or a lover not wanting
to get in too deep.

      Autumn on the way to meet winter
is predictable and steadfast
like geese flying south
and corn losing ground to houses.

      So when autumn winds begin to blow
bring out the down coat.
Lean into the winds
without looking back
and walk into the next season.

Proposal

His image is like
an old faded picture,
the gentle look in his eyes,
noble form of his nose
and small chin.
The intelligence of his speech
stands out
against the blurring of his hearing.
Gentle strength of his touch
when dancing,
draws me close today
while his eyes search the room.
His vitality belongs to a time
spent long ago
that spans like a time tunnel
between us,
a gentle passing in the night,
when what cannot be today
might have been yesterday
if it were not that we lived
so many years apart
and which a thousand carings
cannot change.

Solace

When the late October sun
drops bright raspberry
behind trees
west of the Mississippi,
twilight follows
a disappointed lover
who finds refuge
in the light of the new moon
and the tenderness of night.

Circle of Giving

>(Ref. to Psalms 8, 24, 41, 23)

>Oh Lord, *You have set your glory
>above the heavens.*

Behind tree line,
sun sets tonight,
fiery ball
lighting the sky,
on the path of life.

>*The earth is the Lord's and all that is in it,
>the world and those who live in it.*

He left us stewards
to care for, enjoy and keep it,
for richer or poorer.
When earthquakes shake foundations,
when parched land brings famine,
when unemployment leaves people destitute,
and misfortune or disaster leaves them unable,
let me help – light the candle,
bring food to the table,
clothes to the door,
keys to a place of their own.
Let me help teach the children
that they may learn
to help themselves.

>*Happy are those who
>consider the poor.*

Just as we return
to our parents,
who reared and taught us,
to help us bridge
difficult times,
so we turn to God.
For God rocks
humanity's cradle.

The Lord is my shepherd,
I shall not want.

Giving, we share, in communion
with neighborhood and globe
in the circle of life.
Then the sun will rise tomorrow
with rays of hope
over the lake of new beginnings.

Perpetual Journey

> Just another day
> to hurry through non-stop.

> Between classes in the hall,

platform of a separate world,
students file past in seemingly endless
streams of daily migration,
humming their songs.

> In the windowless room where

air fills with topics for papers
in one class and responses to
"Guten Tag!" and "Wie geht's?"
in another, I dispense tissues
and hand lotion respectively, on request.
Students fill empty space to bursting;
walls partition sights but not sounds.

> Posters are horizon,

Einstein and Beethoven,
and "Write Your Own Dream."
Today's Emily and Walt look forward
unknowing, their faces mirror
in that world where
you know "You're special."

> We travel by air

with Carl Sandburg
under the American flag to the
Berlin of their imaginations,
continue with Alice Walker
past the "November 9," of the year
their wall of inhibitions fell.
They read their papers aloud,
respond to questions,
travel past Switzerland and wall maps

across old boundaries
to changing borders
of the second language,
of language arts and creative writing,
letting their dreams escape across lips
into open air of excitement.

    They seek galaxies
    past old customs and technologies,
    in after school sports,
    drum line and prom,
    in atmosphere of computer games
    and cell phones, breath
    of a rapidly traveling universe.

Surprise

It may as well be Valentine's Day
the way he holds open the door
to the convenience store. The tall
brunette gentleman
with sparkling blue eyes
smiles invitingly. His posture
seems to say I can't wait
to hold you in my arms. I speed
my steps, not to keep him waiting
too long. Returning his smile,
I thank him for holding the door.
And just as I pass, I glimpse
the figure of a slim, long-haired
blond woman coming up
right behind me
and into his waiting arm.

New Season

Autumn leaves
and pumpkin smiles
pale moon at the window

school days
and birthdays
      sun so warm
          roses start to bloom again

birds gathering in trees
plentiful as chestnuts
      all are seeds of a new season

like the smile
of a new friend
across the room

Halloween Spirits

Colors fade in fields,
    specters vanishing in haystacks.
Daylight fades,
    wind blowing cloud veils
    across moon's face.

Flickering jack-o'- lantern
    makes scarecrows dance.
    Halloween sends black mask of unknowing
        in a converging of spirits that roam.
        They resurrect
    incarnation of costumes
        of who they are
    or might be
        in subliminal spell of night
    at doorstep of the unconscious.
Shadows emerge, sainted or diabolic,
    incognito selves
    in ghostly depths of darkness.
        They flit around in misty air
        of mischief and laughter.
    Whimpering ghouls
        of ages past or might-haves
        linger among waiting skeletons.
    Whispering phantoms
        of present or should-haves
        catch in cobweb of memories,
    while snickering witches
        ride brooms into fantasy of will-bes.
    Scheming goblins
        mock attempts to escape the future.
    Roving Harpies
        stir crowd in confusion.
    in the land of the supernatural.

Soon wind of reason threatens
    to blow away stirrings into netherworld,
        like fallen leaves, to compost,
        like nighttime shadows, to fade,
    leaving behind only
    bursting buckets of treats,
    autumn trees graced with garlands of toilet paper,
    and extinguished pumpkin smiles.

November

Sun draws long shadows
of young evergreen trees
across lawn
assembly of spruce and pine
invite into their circle
of prayer
The rust colored maple
in their center
drapes a fallen halo
of leaves
around its trunk
the bare crown
in worship
reaching
up

On Summit Hill

     Granite blocks and mortar,
rounded arches, dome reaching into sky,
the Cathedral of Saint Paul draws me,
like other nameless, faceless souls
into its sphere every time I travel
Kellogg Boulevard to Summit Avenue
and on into the hub of downtown.

     The Cathedral, throne of the Almighty,
reigns over Saint Paul, south of the Capitol;
west of City Hall, library, Union Depot, airport;
east of residential streets, pivotal point
separating the city's public and private sections,
unknown from known, past to present,
north of the Mississippi River.

     In wake of 9/11, the Cathedral, like a mother,
embraces crowd on eve of Thanksgiving as they
follow footsteps of past worshippers into sanctuary
like immigrants who helped build this hallowed place.
They let prayers rise along columns of gold
and black marble, to the angels and Saint Paul,
to domed ceiling of heavenly scenes, Holy Spirit
into gates of hope. We come, seeking answers,
pledge allegiance to our beliefs, wearing
the Stars and Stripes over our hearts. Like a fortress,
the Cathedral receives the community under God,
indivisible: denominations of Christians, Jews,
Moslems, and every faith imaginable, agnostics,
believers, and unbelievers, ethnic groups, and anyone
seeking refuge. We crowd in as into a Noah's Ark
of liberty, regardless of national origin, for direction
and justice for all, one human spirit beneath stars
and spangles of human destiny.

     On the hill –
life of spirit intersects with daily routine – Cathedral
of Saint Paul stands watch over ordinary lives.

Give Us This Day

Once a month the team of Hope take turns
serving our Frogtown neighbors. One by one
we drift into the basement hall of Faith.
Hunger is an equal opportunity state:
yesterday it was I; today it is they,
and, who knows, tomorrow it may be you.
It is like verb conjugation that can affect us all,
depending on who or where we are—and when.

I go, because it is like motherhood
that took its lessons from days
when the sister was left to care
for younger siblings while parents were out.
This impulse of caring for others resurfaced
with the birth of my children and hung on
after they left home. Having expanded
into the community of teaching,
it eventually moved into the community at large
like into an extended family.

At Loaves and Fishes we converge, regardless
of our daytime occupations, as life's stations
dissolve into common purpose where
teacher and businessman, lawyer and accountant,
engineer and minister, chemist and artist,
student and retiree become equal partners,
newly distinguished as set-up crew and preparers,
cooks and servers, dishwashers and clean-up crew
in a return to the basics of living. We function
much as a family does, everyone contributing
with one of the listed jobs. You don't need
a college degree or check book to be there,
just shares of involvement and knowledge
of how pronouns change the meaning of verbs,
such as in I will see you there.

We serve in the line of humanity filing past
and in prayer of fellowship, where each person
becomes part of the whole, worker and diner,
where spaghetti and meat balls satiate more than hunger,

with or without Parmesan cheese, establish a link
with applesauce of community, bread of life,
banana of nurture, and ice cream of friendship.
Second helpings assure no one leaves still wanting,
which opens lively exchanges between us.

After clean-up,
having put life back in order
just like at home,
we leave with the tiredness of knowing
the day now is truly complete. One by one,
we drift back into the rhythm of separate paths,
but I know we all hope to return
on next month's serving day.

Thanksgiving

       We give thanks for
sunny fall days
that allow yellow school bus pansies
to keep blooming

       comfortable shoes
       free elections

fallen leaves descending rust
gold and yellow to form a bridge
into the next season

birthday celebrations
the Pilgrims at Plymouth Rock
       geese flying overhead
dinners with family and friends
conversation over hot cider and pie

       poetry plentiful
       as falling leaves

wall of trees opening vision
past birds and squirrels nests
disclosing scenery marking the land

new roads to explore
new friends to welcome
       evergreen trees standing tall
home and old traditions
work and new challenges

       Beethoven's *Moonlight Sonata*
       dancing all night

walking around the lake
whose waters undulate
grey to emerald green
and watching tall prairie grass
       wave in wind

       picking apples before the frost
       warm sweaters and coats

Union

      for Tom and Nancy Lancaster

When the organ fills the sanctuary
      with octaves
of untold generations
      who enter
through portals of prayer
      to sit
in pews of meditation,
the choir accompanies
the spirit
to the altar of hope and praise
their hymns
uplifting to holy Presence
      in the union
of instrument and voice

Walk to the Center of the Universe

The walk
between picture and word
is a short one.

It is like entering a cathedral
whose sun-lit stained glass windows
absorb the organ's passion,
while the choir's rhythmic voices
trail down the aisle of spirit and soul
to the altar of art,
the bible of creativity,
the bread and chalice of community
in the center of His universe.

The movement
between music and dance
is continuous

in eternal entwining
of spirit and mind,
body and soul
around the winged staff
of artistic creation.

My Father's World

Ageless
Weightless
it extends
beyond sunset
in light of an ever-burning sun
into the next millennium
of infinite space

V. Winter, Storehouse

*If you have built castles in the air, your work
need not be lost; that is where they should be.
Now put the foundations under them.*
              from Walden by Henry David Thoreau

As evenings sink into darkness, we look forward to holiday lights, holy Birth, a white Christmas, and dance into the new year with expectations. Cold winds greet us, but snow brightness makes violets bloom inside window panes as if it were spring. Chickadees dart in evergreen tree. Stocked cupboard and refrigerator see us through blizzards. Skiers capture hills and valleys, and fishermen and hockey players frequent frozen lakes. Icy roads cannot keep us home; lined leather boots, front wheel drive, and determination will get us there.

Each season brings out our resilience and adaptability, sometimes beyond our imagination. They are part of what allows us to carry on the great experiment, part of what gives me something to look forward to in the circle of life, where I always come back to the same places but each time in different ways. So that when winter comes again, it's new, like the fashions. It is just like when I visit somewhere else, another city or country and return, park and lake look different, so do streets and people; even the pulse of traffic feels different. One might ask: Is it because they have changed, or because my perception has changed, or because I truly look at them for the first time? Perhaps it is all of these. But what is it that we really see in our day to day interactions? Whenever I draw a familiar landmark, I am amazed how long it takes me to capture every detail important to my composition. No matter how often I look at it, I see something new, something I did not notice before. And when the light changes, the entire view may change from what I saw before. Similarly, what I believed yesterday, may no longer conform to what I perceive today, because new experiences have changed my outlook or understanding or because the circumstances in which I lived yesterday have changed.

Not surprisingly, we make new year's resolutions, whether we keep them or not. As much as we fear change, we also like it, provided it is not overwhelming. That is because we need to have something to look forward to all the time. And we must live our own vision of life. So we start seedlings for the garden in our basement, clean out a closet and find forgotten treasures of past days. We may plan next summer's home remodeling or a vacation trip. We may join a club, take a course to brighten evening hours. Or we may read a book, start a new hobby, make new friends and find new connections. Some people may go in for a make-over and discover a new image. When I add new activities to my life, I tend to focus on the excitement of the new experience. Perhaps it is the life-long student in me, but as soon as I have mastered or exhausted possibilities of one activity, it is time to take the next step. It is a way to become proficient, a seemingly endless process, so that I am frequently in transition, whether it entails teaching or engaging in the arts. For me, the satisfaction is in the next step, the becoming—the process of expansion and discovery.

In January of my adolescence, I discovered a new world after the family made the voyage across the ocean from Hamburg to New York. We came like pilgrims, knowing mostly that this was the genesis of a new life. No number of adventure books I read could have prepared me for this greatest of adventures. For in this story, I found protagonists were not heroes, though some stood tall, but ordinary people. I was not victor, though I overcame hardships, but observer who morphed into citizen. And after the initial start, a fluffing of feathers and finding our own space, life was life, as natural as a change of clothes or going to the store, to school, to work or—coming home. Life took hold, a transplant, roots and all, the past a mere memory for me, like a dream both frightful and beautiful. I was soon versed in two worlds, though I lived in one, making occasional visits to the other. As Gemini, I travel under Pollux and Castor, protectors of sailors, something I enjoy as symbolic representation of my journey. And one generation of children later, the journey takes new direction across the ocean of imagination and land of experience, past teaching, where newly found territory needs to be recorded, new visions drawn, pioneer-like, in this uncharted journey, where so many directions invite exploration.

We cannot always rely on custom or tradition to draw a map of our progress. Custom and tradition can signal opportunity, stagnation, even impasse, depending on the times and whom we know, and where we want to go. Fashions change seasons. What is the rage one season is out the next, like corsets and stilettos, taking turns to challenge the fashion conscious. Fallen kings of yesterday made room for regular citizens of today. The Civil Rights movement keeps uprooting old thinking in widening circles. Yet democracy has been around at least since ancient Greece. After Orville and Wilbur Wright made their first flight which few thought possible, the skies opened to all the world. Golda Meir came from Russia to America and then became prime minister of Israel, a woman's complex progress. There is a train of thought that frees us to pursue our dreams beyond ordinary or past bounds that lights our way into the future. But it does not always come easily. It is not automatic, nor is there a course of study to lead us there. Yet in Creation we are all children of untold potential.

When my father died in February of his ninety-second year, my mother followed seven months later, less than two weeks before the date of their wedding anniversary, exactly one month short of her ninety-first birthday. Their primary legacy is the model of their lives. Beyond that, my father left us his pictures and genes of imagination, intellect, and talent. My mother left us her work ethic, organizational skills, and appreciation of beauty. Both taught us how to stitch life's pieces together. It is up to us, their children, whether we store, give away, or make use of what we were given to carry life one step forward.

It becomes our task to develop who we are which changes at different stages in life. So when Hollywood hands out leading roles primarily to the young, or industry prefers to hire and promote the young over more experienced employees, we need to take a closer look at the results. Even the young have trouble living up to flawless complexions and super thin bodies in the media. At work the young look to the experienced for mentoring and modeling. Yet we cannot let the vision of someone else's notion of success overshadow our vision of ourselves. Industry and organizations have their goals at heart, goals that change with economic and financial winds. But recent financial failure and economic down-turn show that financial dealings are as much of an art as any other employment, system, or procedure. I do not believe, however, that money alone is a good measure of success in the modern world, though it certainly can be measure of power and influence, and a sufficient amount is necessary for survival. Each age of an individual has something to offer community and world, something without which the whole is left at a disadvantage. When we outsource products, we sacrifice an important source of skills and personal and national identity. The same holds true when we urge early retirement on workers, teachers and other professionals who would prefer to keep working. We are draining our knowledge and experience pool necessary for a well educated, productive society. It can reduce personal opportunity as we were accustomed to it at the same time as it can lower national norm of living. Thus, we need to rethink our approach to life, and it will, likely, bring us to where we wanted to go in the first place.

Youth has its quick intelligence, physical energy, and enthusiasm. The notion that children and teens are necessarily smarter today than they were in the past is myth, though they may be more world-wise. Yet we rarely give them credit for how capable and responsible they can be and many really are. I remember a day when teachers introduced middle school students to computers to motivate them to write their papers. Today students know much about the web, computer games, and social networks. But when it comes to doing research and writing papers, it is the teacher that introduces them to this area. Since they were born into the computer age, they readily accept this world, for it is their world. Not having grown up with technology some adults, particularly older adults, may need to make a special effort to get into things. Lack of exposure and opportunity leave them overwhelmed by the idea. Life experience and maturity make them more cautious with anything new. Obviously, circumstance and posture do play roles heres. However, recent research has shown learning is not just for the young. It can continue lifelong. Indeed, it is beneficial to the brain. Experience, maturity and the tendency to reflect are certainly assets to adult learning, as non-traditional students often discover. Truth is, we need a mix of young and experienced, even older workers, particularly in view of longer life expectancies and consequent economic concerns, to realize our own and our nation's dream that may erode, if these developments remain ignored.

Modern science shows our cells grow and renew, even as we age. Exercise not only transforms bones and muscles but also expands the brain. Life is growth, growth that continues even into middle age and on, so that we can learn a new activity or skill at any age. Without growth, decline takes over on the route of inactivity, from valley of sadness to course of pessimism, until it arrives at a state of infirmity. The antidote, if we can reprogram our thinking, is to do our part on the scale of well being or decline. Good health, in all stages of life, involves four aspects: physical activity, mental challenge, psychological well being, and spiritual involvement. Each of these can stimulate and activate the other, because cells communicate. In other words—the body knows. The mystic, Mechthild von Magdeburg says in her untitled poem: "God endowed all creatures such / that they foster their nature. / How could I then withstand my nature?"

From cradle to grave, there are so many ways to turn life into a creative design. The time is right to reinvent life—and ourselves.

Crossroads

Winter

Freshly fallen snow
        covers frozen lake
a blank page
        waiting
to be written on

Along the Way

Picture windows promise a White Christmas, glistening
tonight beneath street lights, Courier and Ives scene
at W. A. Frost. We meet, three women, incarnation
of childhood recollections of distant beginnings, merged

into adulthood of the here and now. Each of us represents
an aspect of past and present, of my life. We celebrate near
where we first met at St. Paul's Germanic American Institute,
visitor, newcomer, and old resident. We share a heritage,

a varying language, each with a different accent on life,
different perspectives of old and new, here and there,
as we align teaching German with changing times. Once more
we toast with the wine of friendship, enjoy the meal

of common experience – this moment for eternity, the future,
and the departing friend. It is farewell dinner of our meetings
as much as of a period in our lives, as we move on, each
according to our circumstance and design. Blizzard

of transition and good byes obscures our now separate
directions across bridge of two worlds. The German friend
takes the "yes, I can" of the American Dream back
to the old country to partner a new language school there.

The Austrian friend moves into a new financial career
with her American husband in Minneapolis. And I
now teach writing at the Loft and publish my first book.
Each of us is traveling across the horizon of a new dawn,

our regular gatherings soon to fade into the past. Some day
we may converge here again, catch up with each other
in language of a new beat but in summer's garden, across
from Common Good Books, in sequels of our life stories.

Christmas

I Advent

    Christmas, the biggest birthday celebration
of the year—Advent lighting "moments of being"
candle by candle, carol by carol,
sending the soul on a journey
over road of art to manger of faith.

    We look for a way out of darkness' isolation
and follow Christmas lights and traffic
into malls and shops, advertising entreating
our wish to give and to have—
while Christmas bells ring for
the poor, the destitute, the shut-ins.

    Christmas is the destination where we arrive
by phone, card or e-mail, by transport or foot and—
or by memory—on the annual pilgrimage to our
connection, our roots. Pieces of the puzzle
called self fall into place when we arrive,
fill in the picture that is our life.

    We follow the Spirit to gatherings,
overtaking business and workday worlds, where,
for the time being, we become of one mind,
reaching out across round tables of peace
and friendship in the circle of colleagues
and friends, the shelter of our families.

II Old Traditions

    Old traditions flash back, like Dad bringing
the tree home Christmas Eve day and we
children trimming it with him, jumping with joy
once we all gathered around the decorated,
lighted tree. Then we searched among gifts
for that treasured plate of Christmas goodies.

    When my brothers and I married, the
tradition changed. Every year my husband and I

made the 330-mile trip to Milwaukee to my parents'
house with our two small children over snow
and ice, in sunshine or darkness, never faltering,
rarely missing a year—guided by the Christmas Wish.

    Greeted with embraces and kisses at the door,
Dad's cooking and Mom's baking received us back
into their world, my other siblings and their families
filling the house to overflowing. Dad would say
with a sigh: "So, the family is together again."

III Celebration

    When I decorate the tree, I begin with angels
disburse them evenly, like the red, sparkly one
from my mother, or the ones playing musical
instruments from Germany, the string ones
made by a colleague, the glass ones
with gold wings from a friend –

    I continue with porcelain dove from another
teaching buddy; glass wreath from a student;
crystal ornament from my daughter; the wise men,
only two left now, my son made in elementary
school; last year's Snoopy and other wooden toy
and bell ornaments in a seemingly endless array –

    Then it's time to be off to the Tableaux Service
that refills the Spirit's cup and lets imagination
rise like the incense carried by magi in their
procession down the center aisle of expectation
in light of candles of prayers to mystical
communion, gift of the season.

    The new tradition for my children is to spend
Christmas Day at my house, since grandparents
are gone. Just like the tree is link to the past,
ornament by ornament, our link to continuity
comes story by story to which we will add
perhaps another this year to remember next year.

Communion around dinner table, sound
of Christmas carols in background is the gift we
share over the meal of conversation and wine
of our bond in rounds of who did what, when,
of revelations, aspirations, future dreams, ending
in confusion and laughter of gift exchange.

Only the Christmas story remains one and
the same for us to lean on every year
as we look for signs,
and we listen attentively,
each time as for the very first time.

IV The Future

From darkness and emptiness of decreasing
days, advent moves us forward with each
candle lit to Birth of Joy and Light of Peace
into expanding days of Hope.
Christmas makes life new again each year.

Gifts to my Children

    This country,
bigger than imagination, more varied
than seasons, diverse as the people who
live here without rumble and flames of war
is my legacy, gift to my children.

    In a house built on love
with a room of everyone's own, toy chests
packed with dreams, bookshelves filled
with wonders and adventures, closets holding
personalities of new possibilities,
refrigerator and cupboards always stocked,
large windows offer view to a promising future.

    Connection to grandparents,
aunts, uncles, and cousins over time and distance
keeps them linked to source and nature of their
being to help recognize themselves as parts
of the whole, to guide them through childhood
wonder and play into adulthood of their own
making, like children of pioneers.

    The children have a lifetime of chances
to attend open schools of opportunity, develop
talents as varied as their imaginations
to follow options or answer callings,
prepare for vocations that hold keys
to their own choices, world of their future.

    Their lives advance with friends
who pull them into their surroundings,
marking who they become for the occasion,
the experience, or the whole journey.

    Within limits of their environs,
they can disappear into a crowd
or build their future on a stage,
not to a ready blueprint of tradition
but to their own specifications, past bounds
of the known into expanse of the unknown

by means of their capabilities and drive
as pastime or experiment or
accomplishment of a lifetime.

    Not wrapped or boxed, these gifts
are not certificates, to be redeemed later.
Nor have they been charged, to be paid
as you go, nor funded with loans. These gifts
are there for the taking – good for a lifetime.

    Given freely,
they come straight from the heart,
foundation and head start, inalienable,
birthright of the new order of things.

    The gifts are yours,
without road map or directions, regardless
of weather. Hope and faith can lay out the plan.
Skill provides the vehicle for traveling roads
of ingenuity and hard work that brought
the family to this place, ready to take
the driver into the future. Love lights
the way beyond present into dawn and day,
success of your own space voyage.

    This, my gift, is your future.
All you need to do is set and keep
your own course in rhythm
with the wave of your millennium.

New Year's Prayer

Let
the new year
create order out of chaos
wholeness out of brokenness
direction out of doubt

Let
us gather
'round the table of humanity
with centerpiece
of seedling plant
where the poor are rich in spirit
and the powerful generous in deed
where the sick are healed
and the lonely uplifted
where the lost are found
and the wayward return

Let us
fill the bowl
with soup of understanding
eat buttered bread of compassion
raise the cup
with milk of love
and toast old bonds
pray for new beginnings
in the new year's
increasing light

Let us sing
hymns of tolerance
in the circle of this diverse world
let bells of peace and joy
declare our resolution

Amen

Out of the Past

On a windy Super Bowl Sunday in St. Paul, cars
suddenly line freeway onto exit ramp, rush hour style.

In the distance, the Ice Castle, made of blocks
hewn from lake of wishes, glows ghostly blue
in a harbor of incandescent street lamps. Its walls
release colored lights that explode to music, drawing
onlookers into translucent childhood dreams,
where fairy godmothers watch over children,
and witches live in remote forests;
where princess sleep all day, and frogs turn princesses;
where swords have healing powers, and kings
conduct just wars, somewhere far away;
where plagues won't fall from a burning sky;
where benevolent despots help the poor
and ban offenders to the tower of no vision.
There little girls are called to be lawyers,
engineers or cheerleaders and little boys choose
to be football, hockey or movie stars or poets.
There stars fall to earth gold coins, princess
slays fire-breathing dragon to win prince,
and they live separately ever after
in polarity of a debt-free kingdom.

February shadows recall uncounted spirits,
soon to be released back into the lake,
that some distant day they may resurface
to haunt anew the merry-go-round of life.

Toby's on the Lake

It's gone—our landmark, birthplace of memories –
erased from the street, as if life were just a dream.

From above roof line, the sign once read:
"Toby's on the Lake." Cars dropped passengers
under arched roof at the entrance. Inside,
reception room waited with cushioned benches
along windows. Walls drew guests into pictures,
scenes of boats and boating and British royals.
January snow now covers the lot like a moonscape.

First time at Toby's, I saw the 3M crowd attired
in business suits and computer ties and knee-length
dresses, milling around in dining room and bar,
standing room only. Later, we came to celebrate
birthdays, anniversaries, friendships, or a night out.
The owner circulated between tables,
a welcoming host. If we were lucky, we sat
by the fireplace, watched words dance among embers,
or by the window, letting conversation drift
across lake. Weekend nights, piano accompanied
communion. In summer, terraced patio invited
to umbrella tables amid potted flowers, swimmers
and beach-goers moving through our stories
far side of Tanners Lake.

Last time, I was to meet an old friend for dinner. But
by then it was "Donovan's." Scenic pictures were gone
from walls the way the royal yacht was retired
in Britain. It was cash or credit card only.
When my friend did not arrive, a quick call
brought her out forty-five minutes later, wearing a smile
that said she had not forgotten the friendship.

Toby's on the Lake is gone – empty space stunted
by struggling economy of a city that keeps
rebuilding itself. We follow the tracks half a step
behind in snow of change, as if the past needs
obliterating in transforming landscapes of our lives.

Visits in Highland Park

We met in college in Milwaukee, when she used to come over
for coffee after school. In following years, we moved, first she
to Saint Paul, where she taught, then I and my husband to Minneapolis.
We would talk endlessly on the phone about teaching and sewing,
and of the dream to own a home some day. Soon my friend,

Lee, and her husband, Jerry, bought a house in Highland Park. This older
home had a landscaped yard with golf grass like a carpet. They thrived
on cultivating the garden a little more each season, energy of their ideas.
They added more flowers and shrubs, rock garden and shade trees, vines,
pond, and, yes, more land. They wanted to build their gazebo
on the wooded lot. And not to forget, they work a hidden vegetable patch.

At her house in summer, visit becomes walk in the park—which they
tend like a living room, with something new to discover each time.
Their garden attracts State Horticultural Society crowd and *Northern
Gardener* journalist alike as well as bus loads of gardening enthusiasts
from all over, the hosts' punch-bowl hospitality always ready to welcome
the groups of visitors touring their garden every season.

In autumn, you can find them raking and bagging leaves in nearby parks
to make sure there is enough mulch, always willing to share a bag or two.
In winter, they order seeds and plan and plant in their basement
and green house to be ready in time for spring planting.

As if that were not enough, in winter, she braids rugs with strong
gardener hands in spare time. She learned the craft from an aging aunt
many years ago, braiding strips of old garments, like the poetry
of memories, into colorful rugs, bright greens and blues, reds, yellows,
and whites. It is as though she moves the American Dream from outdoors
indoors in those months. These Early American, rugs warm any room,
prize winners at State Fairs, legacy of history—her legacy—like
the homestead. The rugs invite to step inside and feel at home any time.

And when she makes jams and jellies to die for and meals that include
every fresh vegetable in her garden and more, served with talk
of gardening and birds—and African violets, all the while feet rest
on braided rugs of pioneering spirit, it is her Dream—
the American Dream—brought into twenty-first century living.

Snowscape

From light grey sky,
snow flakes gently dance
in circles
over Markgrafs Lake
as if the day
were but a myth

lake and streets
rows of identical
light colored houses
lie bedded
beneath Persephone's blanket
of white stillness
resembling a dream
where we cannot find
our way

here and there
would-be landmarks prompt
our direction
barren trees
white tufted evergreens
harboring chickadees
draw the eye
in snowscape that dazes

perhaps the road's curve
will guide us home

Retreat at the Benedictine Center

Our lives come together
like trains
in the railroad yard

parallel lives
intersect
at intervals
then carry out
their parallel journeys

we traverse the same state
the same continent
time and again
each carrying our load

only when we empty
the cargo
do we recognize the pieces
each carrying a share
that makes up the whole

with newfound solidarity
we disperse again
in different directions
to keep up our ends
raised to new heights
in the changing world
of ordinary lives

The Labyrinth

We travel the daily labyrinth
like a road into the fog

knowing only it stretches
infinitely up ahead
forward only forward
we bring wishes like prayers
our agenda like a plan
but we follow the road
share the space with fellow travelers
greet our friends along the way
as we get used to the turns
that seemingly send us
in different directions
we travel the circular route
find God's Spirit at the core
travel becomes easier as we
open heart and mind
to the joy of the journey
prayers lightening load
hymns speeding step

We travel our road
a labyrinth into the light

February Fog

February fog rises
spirit over Mississippi,
Saint Paul's river,
like thoughts of spring
and river boat excursions
of past summers.
The river remains captive
beneath veiled fingers of ice.

Valentine

Thoughts of you
entrance
like spring flowers
filling days spent apart

you are the stem
that connects
the roots
that nourish

you add color
to gray hours
harmony
to discordant days

Thoughts of you
refresh
like spring rain
saturating the soil
of our connection

The Plumber

    She will arrive shortly, the dispatcher says,
as I envision a stocky, middle aged woman
with short-cropped hair and raspy voice.

    When the door bell rings, a slim young woman
of medium height appears at the door, a brunette
with long wavy ponytail beneath plumber's cap,
carrying a large tool bag. Large hazel eyes smile
at me as she investigates plumbing requirements.
She removes old faucet and cuts new pipe
with the precision of a surgeon, installs and wipes
new faucet with the care of a proud homeowner.

    "I never met a woman plumber before," I say.
"Neither have I," she chuckles from below the sink,
her voice strong as though speaking over
running water. "The bathroom fixture
won't take quite so long she says, carrying
defective water purifying tank outside,
dumping it onto the lawn to drain like a cyst.
She replaces bathroom fixture with the ease
of those who have done it before.

    "What a handy skill for a woman to have,"
I remark and offer her cake and coke to top off the job.
Hesitant to sit down, she eats standing up, as if
the next appointment tugged at her arm like the tools
she gathers into her bag. I sign paper like a new age
agreement of sorts. We shake hands at the door.

    I watch her walk to her truck with a memory
taking me back many years, when an eighth grade girl
in my class, despite tears running down her face,
was not allowed to take geometry with the boys,
because girls had sewing during that time, instead.

    Once more I examine finished work.
Leak free, trim, shiny faucet and fixture
have, at last, renewed kitchen and bathroom—and life,
improvements a long time in coming.

In February Light

      For many years
the philodendron sent lush trails
like flourishes
down the buffet's edge

      gradually
leaves spot brown and fall
exposing long bare stems
I cannot figure why

      taking cuttings
of remaining leaders
I wash and rinse
place them in water

      stems soon drive new roots
new leaves begin to form
and I plant rooted cuttings
in fresh soil

      within days
new shiny green leaves
spill over edges
of the flower pot

      in hope
of February light
life sometimes needs to start over
not from seed
but from the rib
somewhere past mid-point

Friendship

Friendship is the violet
that blooms
even in the dead of winter

Lenten Journey

      (from Psalm 121)

   I lift my eyes to the hills—

This time of lent
is born of spirit
baptized
in the river of the journey

I head into the wilderness
of transition
breaking continuity
of familiar structure and days

Longing
moves me into the future
over hills and valleys
of promise and disappointment
to seek the river's source

   My help comes from the Lord

I pray for endurance
to find my way through the forest
of doubt and bewilderment

for faith
to walk the path past the canyon
of ignorance

for wisdom
to distinguish
between mirage and vision

   The Lord is your keeper

I pray for inspiration
to lead me
to headwaters of life's river
and travel the current
to the Easter of new purpose

Cycle of Creation

Across a wasteland
       past memories

into the reaches
       of outer space

each night is a star
       to wish upon

each day the light
       of creation

Finding the Way

What if the house were a ship
traveling the ocean of snow waves
through the gale of indecision
to the calm of sunrise
along the horizon of inspiration
to a new land
there for the voyager to disembark
discover new vistas
explore mountains and valleys
traverse unrelenting deserts
and forests with deer tracks and chickadees
follow the rivers and cross the lakes
watch blue heron and butterfly return
to a world close as spring time
that once seemed unreachable

References

Anthology of German Verse. Faber du Faur von, Curt and Kurt Wolff. Pantheon: New York, New York, 1949.
    Goethe, Johann Wolfgang, "An den Mond," 168-169.
    Magdeburg, Mechthild von. "Der Fisch kann in dem Wasser nicht ertrinken," 30.
    Rilke, Rainer Maria. "Ich lebe mein Leben in wachsenden Ringen," 444.

Dickinson, Emily. Johnson, Thomas H., Ed. *The Complete Poems of Emily Dickinson*. Little Brown and Company: Boston, 1960, 657.

Jung, C. G., *Aspects of the Masculine*, R.F.C. Hull, Transl. Princeton University Press: Princeton, New Jersey, 1989.

**Modern British Literature*. Kermode Frank, and John Hollanders, Eds. Oxford University Press: London, 1973.
    Auden, W.H., "The Watershed," "The Unknown Citizen."
    Browning, Robert, "My Last Duchess."
    Tennyson, Alfred Lord, "Lady of Shalott," "Ulysses."
    Thomas, Dylan, "Fern Hill."
        "The force that through this green fuse drives the flower."
    Yeats, William Butler, "The Second Coming."

Greene, Graham. *The Power and the Glory*. Penguin Books: New York, 1971.

Woolf, Virginia. *To the Lighthouse*. Harcourt Brace Jovanovich: New York, 1955.
    Mrs. Dolloway. Harourt Brace Jovanovich: New York, 1953.

Plato. *Theatetus*. Benjamin Joett, Transl., 12. http://classics.mit.edu/Plato/theatetu.html

The Author

Evelyn Klein's writing is a venture from reality into imagination. One path exposes topics of interest and concern in the language of prose. The other explores ideas with the sensibility, metaphor and succinctness of poetry. Her drawings help set the scene.

Evelyn's poetry and articles have appeared in numerous journals, anthologies, newspapers, and other publications. In 1994, she published the anthology Stage Two: Poetic Lives, illustrated by her father. In 2005 her poem "A Place Called Home" was a prize winner with the Family Housing Fund in Minneapolis and is still touring the Twin Cities in an exhibit of art and poetry. In 2006, she published her first book of poetry, a memoir in verse, *From Here Across the Bridge*, with art by her father, Wolfgang Klein. The book won a cover award with the Midwest Independent Book Publishers. In 2009, she published her second book of poetry, prose and her own drawings, *Once upon a Neighborhood*, part history, memoir, and observation. It has been placed in the Minnesota Historical Society's permanent library collection.

The author, mother of two grown children, has lived most of her life in the Twin Cities of Minnesota and surrounding area. She has traveled extensively in Europe and in the United States. Born in Berlin, Germany, she spent her formative years in Milwaukee. She earned a B.S. in Secondary Education at the University of Wisconsin-Milwaukee and an M.S. in the Teaching of English at the University of Wisconsin-River Falls. Klein taught German and English literature and writing in the public schools of Wisconsin and Minnesota for many years. She led a poetry group at the Loft and, subsequently taught at the Loft and at Century College. She is a freelance writer, speaker, editor, and writing judge who, more recently also, became a visual artist.